MICHAEL SADLER once wrote a doctoral thesis on the failure of the French Symbolist poets to write fiction. He has since managed marginally better himself. His work includes writing for BBC Radio 3 and television, a history of music in strip cartoons, a French art-house film starring Jean-Louis Trintignant and translations of Marivaux for the BBC/RSC. In 2002–3 he adapted Terry Johnson's *Hysteria* for John Malkovich's production at the Théâtre Marigny in Paris. He teaches French at the British Institute in Paris, where he runs an MA course in Contemporary French Studies. He likes Schubert, Led Zeppelin and, if he ever had the chance to taste it, Château Pétrus. He lives in Paris and the Touraine. He has a French wife, a French–English daughter and grows his own leeks.

Also by Michael Sadler

AN ENGLISHMAN IN PARIS

An Englishman
à la Campagne

Life in Deepest France

Michael Sadler

**POCKET
BOOKS**

LONDON • NEW YORK • SYDNEY • TORONTO

First published in Great Britain in 2004
by Simon & Schuster UK Ltd
This edition first published by Pocket Books, 2005
An imprint of Simon & Schuster UK Ltd
A Viacom company

First published in France in 2003
as *Un Anglais à la campagne* by L'Archipel

1 3 5 7 9 10 8 6 4 2

Simon & Schuster UK Ltd
Africa House
64–78 Kingsway
London WC2B 6AH

Simon & Schuster Australia
Sydney

www.simonsays.co.uk

A CIP catalogue for this book is available
from the British Library.

ISBN: 0-7434-9240-4
EAN: 9780743492409

Typeset by Palimpsest Book Production Limited, Polmont, Stirlingshire
Printed and bound in Great Britain by
Cox & Wyman Ltd, Reading, Berkshire

For Lulu and Daisy

1

'*Excusez-nous, monsieur . . .*'

The English leek abroad is impeccably mannered.

'*On est mous!*'

Limp? A quick glance over my left shoulder. The leek plants on the back seat did look a little flabby. Travelling with a band of pubescent vegetables is a tricky business. During the Newhaven–Dieppe crossing, I had walked them on the upper deck wrapped in a Kleenex soaked in Evian water. In the hotel outside Alençon, they were put to bed on the window-sill in the plastic toothbrush cup normally used for serving yourself a nightcap of cooking calva. Unfortunately I woke up late and the leeks had suffered the full blast of the morning sun. Speed was essential. I decided, even if it meant switching veg, to *titiller le champignon* – tickle the mushroom, or put one's foot down.

'*Grouillez-vous.*' The leeks were insistent. 'Please.'

I was hurrying as fast as I could.

The roadmap was sellotaped to the dashboard of the red Mazda. In the village of Toison, population 216, I was to leave the D129, turning left after the church, down the hill past the café, the Toison d'Or – the Golden Fleece – with its mobile Miko ice-cream sign swinging in the breeze. A few hundred yards out of the village, a left turn at a rusty roadside shrine, up the hill, and a right turn at the large municipal bins – a mattress in the yellow one and its springs in the green. Then, straight on past a field of rape and the meticulously manicured hornbeam hedge of an obsessive maths teacher, up a path bordered by wild cherry trees and . . . I've arrived.

My heart beat faster. After all these months, after all that dreaming, my new home. *Enfin!*

I extracted myself with difficulty from the car, a little stiff after the journey from the Orne. In the neighbouring field three cows, who seemed to be looking for their contact lenses in the grass, looked up before resuming their search, in no way interested in the red Mazda driven by a crumpled Englishman in summer tweeds.

The house, true to the photograph I had long fantasised about in Abesbury, was a *longère* – a long, low, white limestone, red-tiled paradise. Different levels of roof distinguished the original components – kitchen, pigsty, stable, living quarters, barn, cellar. The battered oak shutters, with their small cut-out hearts, were like heavy lids on the sleepy windows. A few fat bees in the vine added a soundtrack of somnolence. It was a dream come true.

'Pssst . . .'

The leeks were still uppity. I parked the stroppy bunch in the shade under a large cherry tree and went down to inspect the vegetable garden with its view over the village and the distant spire of Toison. A pretty wooden gate came away in my hands, the rusty hinge denting the helmet of a passing snail. I closed my eyes, savouring the moment. Before me, my new domain. Then I opened them.

Nom d'un chien! I'd been expecting the garden of Eden: I was faced with a jungle. I'd been naïve. The odd weed was, yes, inevitable – the place had been untended for a certain time. But this! The garden had turned Amazonian. Everything had bolted and gone to seed. Six-foot-high lettuces rubbed shoulders with what were once cabbages and what were now flowery parasols for a couple of sardonic rabbits who eyed me, grinning, before slipping back into the security of the undergrowth.

The Dunkirk spirit rose to the surface. This was a

challenge. My new neighbours were going to judge me on my ability to tame the wilderness. *Ils allaient voir.* I'd show them.

Propped against a dilapidated part of the stone garden wall, a scythe. I have never scythed in my life but I remember seeing Yves Montand do it in *Manon des Sources* on BBC2. With this model in mind I lifted the implement, intent on using Marcel Pagnol as a gardening manual. I took the handle in both hands and effected a sweeping gesture. The rusty metal bit flew off into the jungle. In a shed at the top of the garden I found an old spade. I tried digging. The earth was like concrete. I'd not even made a dent.

'Michael . . .'

The lecks were on their last legs. Time was short.

A movement at the bottom of the garden behind the hornbeam hedge. Aimé Matou, my new neighbour, was observing my progress. He was pretending to count the flies around the hindquarters of a cow. But it was not the cow, it was the *roshif* that was the centre of his attention. From the safety of a handy rump he was spying on me. Worse, he was having a quiet laugh.

So as not give the impression that I was intimidated by the task in hand, I retired to the shade of the cherry tree for lunch: *saucisson*, baguette, tomatoes, and a sentimental Livarot purchased in Dieppe high street – a cheese which, because of its very distinctive personality, I had taken the trouble of encasing within a plastic box encased within a second larger plastic box to avoid unfortunate side effects such as death by suffocation. Last but not least, a rather creamy nun – *une religieuse*.

Ddddrrrrrr

What the . . . ?! A terrible noise was coming from behind the wall the other side of the courtyard. I must have nodded off. At the top of the drive, parked directly behind the Mazda, was a large white van with its back door open:

Eric Moineau, électricité générale. I traced the long black rubber lead of the pneumatic drill over to the barn opposite, where Eric Moineau in person was installing a boiler for the future guest flat. I introduced myself.

Monsieur Moineau was young, tallish and wiry, with a smile on his face which seemed to conceal some kind of inner anguish. He worked too quickly, dropped things, and often ran back to the van because he'd got the wrong socket. When you shook his hand you immediately knew what *électricité générale* meant.

To get away from the din I left to explore the house. The entrance was a double door in weather-beaten old wood. The large central room with its faded old red tiles, oak beams and large open fireplace was bathed in the dappled light from the heart-shaped shutters. *Ddddrrrrr.* From the beams hung wicker baskets full of dried flowers. *Ddddrrrrr.* The furniture was a deep honey colour. *Ddddrrrrr.* The bookcases full of leather-bound *ddddr-rrrrr.* All was, as Baudelaire would have had it, *Luxe ddddr-rrrrr calme ddddrrrrrr et volupté. Ddddrrrrrrddddrrr . . .*

Monsieur Moineau was beginning to get up my nose.

Suddenly, a delicious moment of silence. A mobile phone played an electronic snippet from the Choral Symphony. Eric replied, grunted, hung up, ran to his van and reversed down the drive at speed, leaving behind him a cloud of dust which made the cows cough.

In his absence I decided to hide the drill. I crossed the courtyard to the barn, picked up the instrument of torture and stopped. *Eureka.* What a clever idea!

Aimé Matou was still loitering in his field. He was now going through the motions of tinkering with the vertical exhaust pipe of his tractor – an old yellow Renault which he probably bought in a jumble sale during the Russian Revolution. I wanted him to see this. I picked up the drill.

Ddddrrrrr

Aimé's spanner faltered in mid-air.

Ddddrrrrrr

He looked back over his shoulder to the vegetable garden. *Mais . . .* What's he up to? *C'est pas vrai!*

Ddddrrrrrr

Nom d'une pipe!

I placed the pneumatic drill at the beginning of the row. *Ddddrrrrrr.* A hole in the ground. *Plop.* A leek in the hole. *Slurp.* A splash from the watering can. *Phew.* A relieved leek. *Ddddrrrrrr, plop, slurp, phew.* The whole lot are planted in five minutes. The leeks already look much rosier.

Job done, I looked up nonchalantly. Aimé was back behind his rump, holding on to the tail of the cow like a dazed man keeping his balance on a bus. He'd never seen gardening like that before. He looked at the cow, the cow looked at him. They shrugged.

Ils sont fous, ces Anglais!

2

Why the vegetable psychodrama?

Back in England after my first year in Paris,[*] I missed France. The beery bonhomie of the King's Arms left me cold. The smell of stale chip fat and pipe tobacco had lost its edge. I made myself extra-concentrated slugs of continental roast that were so strong they didn't need a cup to stand up in. A video library in Swindon had a few scratched copies of *Nouvelle Vague* movies. I watched them inside out. It wasn't the story I was interested in, it was the décor: the cafés, the streets, the apartments, the dark staircases, the dank courtyards, the bird cages on the window-sills. I listened to the music and imagined the smells: garlic, Gauloises, warm baguettes, wafts of 'Je Reviens'. Which was, of course, what I yearned to do.

But however much I loved Paris, there was another France I wanted to know. There is an expression, a description of a less stressful, more ancestral, old-style, slow-cooking, gently unfolding France that I have always found attractive: *la France profonde* – deepest France, deep as in draught, south, and, maybe, trouble. I was willing to take the risk. I'd taken my first steps as a *parisien*. I now wanted to be a *paysan*.

Desire is the mother of invention. I had been invited to dinner in Abesbury by two colleagues from the University

[*] See *An Englishman in Paris* (Pocket Books, 2003).

of Swindon – Sophie and Malcolm Hodge. Malcolm, a specialist in medieval literature, looked like a self-effacing rodent, with small prominent teeth and a sparse moustache. Sophie was more like Tintin's Castafiore. In her loud, flowery Laura Ashley dresses, she reminded me of an authoritative sofa. The only thing the two had in common was the moustache.

The Hodges had recently acquired the Englishman's dream – a cottage in the Loire valley, a region renowned for being *le jardin de la France*, and the area where the purest French is spoken. In the seventeenth century it was the playground of kings. It was here that they built their extravagant second homes – Chambord, Chenonceaux, Azay le Rideau – and it was here that they spoke their elegant French. Over the years the courtly dialect has rubbed off on the locals. But the Hodges were not to stay to learn it. Malcolm was off to a visiting professorship in Hong Kong. Who was going to take care of their cottage? Who was going to take care of the vegetable garden?

'*Ah! Le potager . . .*'

Sophie's eyes became blurred and moist. She waxed lyrical about the butter beans – '*Oh! Les haricots beurre . . .*' To step out into the garden in the early morning and to bite the taut bottom of a sunfilled tomato . . . The sofa shivered with delight. Emotion was at its height. I decided to join in.

'J'adore les potagers!'

I didn't have the slightest idea what I was talking about. I had once started a tentative vegetable plot in the garden of the cottage I rented in Abesbury. I grew tomatoes in yellow growbags into which I shoved bamboo poles which collapsed every time I watered them, with the result that by the end of the summer I had walked on more fruit than I had eaten. The local branch of the Democratic Union of Slugs voted to leave me the 30 per cent of the carrots I was due. I photographed the survivors for posterity. The high spot was the miniature lettuce patch. I pricked out my dwarf Tom Thumb lettuces to write my name: M-I-C-H-A-E-L. The only problem was that I couldn't bring myself to eat them. Not so the slugs. One morning I woke up to be confronted with a seedbed which spelt out M-I-C-H-A——. Not wanting the neighbours to think I was besotted with a Scandinavian air hostess, I had the lot for lunch.

The Hodges at first thought they had stumbled on the ideal gardener in the person of their neighbour Aimé Matou. But in their absence, Aimé had cut down two old elm trees at the bottom of the garden which were stunting the growth of his barley. This crime opened wounds left by Joan of Arc, the Hundred Years War, Mary Queen of Scots, Trafalgar and Zidane's second goal in the last England–France international. Another gardener had to be found – *illico* – at once.

I had recently bought a second-hand gardening manual at a charity sale in the village hall in aid of pets abandoned by divorcees. Inspired by a fiery Bulgarian red and my desire to return to France I put my new-found knowledge to use. I rushed into the breach, and, snatching the *poireaux vinaigrette* which was served as a starter, grabbed a leek by the shoulder.

'Just look at this leek!'

The other guests were taken aback. Why molest a leek? Using my unoccupied left hand to hammer out my points on the mahogany table, I made an impassioned plea.

'The supermarkets offer a dire picture. Have you ever taken time to peruse the modern leek? What a sight! Spindly and pale, it looks more like an American tourist on growth hormones than a vegetable. Let us never forget: a true leek is squat.'

Then, lapsing into rhetorical French: '*Vive le* Musselburgh! *Vive le* Wroxton! *Vive le* squatness.'

'Squatness' is doubtless not French, but what the

outburst lacked in vocabulary it gained in emotion. The company was enchanted. Such passion! Mrs Hodge, who on that evening was ensconced in a pink concoction which seemed to depict dancing carrots (in fact, when I found my glasses, autumn leaves in the wind), was entranced to play hostess to an ambassador of the traditional vegetable. Her moustache quivered with excitement.

'Michael. *Comme c'est fascinant.*'

My Machiavellian legumery paid off. Two days later a phone call. Sophie Hodge was waiting for me in the tea rooms in Abesbury, this time resplendent in a brown tent decorated with mad cows (I couldn't find my glasses). The glint in her eye indicated she had a plan.

'Michael. *J'ai une petite proposition.*'

She was so happy with her idea. *Moi aussi.*

All that remained to be done was to win over the University of Swindon. Richard Badger, the unctuous and ambitious new Head of Department, who had blond highlights and a Porsche, looked askance at my escapades. Buggering off to France again? What was all this? What was wrong with Britain? Didn't I like tea and rain? Treason was in the air. If I'd told him I'd bought a Harley Davidson and a bandana and that I was going to do Route 66 singing 'Knocking on Heaven's Door' I sense he would have been more compassionate. But France . . . *Le vieil ennemi* . . .

After a certain amount of tedious wheeler-dealing we came to an agreement. Yes, I could go – but this time for one term only – and without salary. I would just have to make do. If the charms of the continent were so great I should be made to suffer for them.

Lu et approuvé. Contract agreed.

I bought a bunch of Musselburgh travelling leeks at the WI market and, with joy and trepidation, once again set about stuffing my gear into the boot of the Mazda. The

Hodges were flying off to Hong Kong, and I to *la France profonde*.

    A nous deux maintenant.

3

Au boulot. Down to work.

I had two small ads to compose. The first was pretty simple – the gist: 'Teacher, English national, Oxford-educated, will give private lessons, telephone etc.'. All the ads on the board in the local Atac supermaket were abbreviated, however. I was none too sure how to abbreviate in French, but designed the following: 'Prof. de nat. angl. dipl. d'Oxf. donne cours, tél: 02 47 59 39 37.'

The second ad was of a more intimate nature, and would require further thought and research.

Atac is situated on the outskirts of the nearest market town, Ligueil. I had often dreamed of Ligueil and Toison, repeating their names like a mantra while standing at the compost at the bottom of the garden in Abesbury. *Ligueil et Toison* ... the names conjured up a magical world tucked away somewhere between Loches and Tours, between Chambord and Ussé, between Vouvray and Chinon, between happiness and bliss. On the kitchen table, the *Atlas Routier Michelin* open at page 82 under the glare of the 100-watt bulb, I would trace the D95 which links the two towns. Today, heart beating fast, no longer pestered by whining leeks, the Mazda is going to replace my finger.

Toison is so small that if you're not careful you're out before you've realised you're in. I turned back on my tracks. The village is composed of three small streets and the Place de l'Eglise – the whole forming a compact diamond shape. There is a bakery and a café, the Toison d'Or. A large sign on the gable end of an old house advertises the direction of the Centre Leclerc in Loches. The municipal handyman and his cart slowly toured the *bourg* in search of a leaf to pick up. A large gentleman with a bulbous purple nose sat outside his house, contemplating nothingness. Three squat ladies with moustaches – Sophie Hodge must have set the fashion – were in discussion in front of the church. All three were wearing orange crash helmets advertising a brand of brake fluid. I slowed down to salute them but they stared at me suspiciously from under their visors and did nothing to acknowledge my cheery wave.

Once you leave the village a steep climb takes you up on to the road leading to Ligueil on the other side of the valley. Some thirty years ago the countryside had been rationalised by a process called *le remembrement*, which involved the tearing up of hedgerows to reorganise and redistribute land. But the patchwork still remains and the landscape is peppered with small farms with their flat red-tiled roofs. Slates stop north of the Loire. Second homes are identifiable from afar by their closed Ronsealed shutters. Otherwise the small houses are real farms with tractors, age-old combine harvesters, fluorescent geraniums and dogs.

In England the exodus from the countryside to the towns began at the end of the eighteenth century. You shut down the farm, kissed the grandparents goodbye and, bag on your shoulder, children under your arm, wife by your side, set off to lose health and happiness in the newly sprawling towns of the Industrial Revolution. As soon as you disappeared over the horizon, the big landowners moved in. It was the end of an era and the last of the peasants. Not so in France. In France, at the same time, things took a different turn. The French Revolution, by giving rights of property to those who used to work for the feudal high and mighty, transformed the peasantry into a political force – because, on the whole, landowners could vote. This had the effect of freezing the countryside into a jigsaw of smallholdings, which explains why the *paysan* survives – if only by the skin of his teeth.

Pardi!

I recently purchased a book by Gérard Granval, *Old Dialects of the Touraine*, published by the Editions de l'Enclume. I had learned a reasonable smattering of the language in Paris but there was no question of talking smart-arse French in *la France profonde*. I've got as far as page 135: peasant exclamations. In using the common ejaculation *'Pardi'* – a derivative of *par Dieu* – I had a quick glance at the position of my lips in the driving mirror with the result that I nearly collided with a lorry carrying huge coils of hay, looking like giant Shredded Wheat, which was leaving Ligueil on the Loches road.

'Morquenne!' (Page 128, lesson 3.)

The town council of Ligueil, or the Ligueilian (Ligalician, Ligamental? – I must ask) town council had the astute idea of putting six parking places on the main street which runs through the town. The result is that it takes on average thirty-three minutes to drive through a town of some two thousand inhabitants. This technique of the artificially induced traffic jam is most effective. The tourist visits the town without being able to leave the car, thus doing away with the need for expensive public car parks. On my way to Atac I had time to admire the Maison Josselyne, corset-maker and supplier of lingerie to the larger lady, whose shop is conveniently placed next door to a specialist in *rillettes*. The proximity is no coincidence. You stuff your face with pâté, wipe your hands on your apron and go next door to hide the fact that you've just made a pig of yourself. The showroom window of chez Josselyne is filled with magnificent satin contraptions. The complex buckles, ties and stays would doubtless have made this shop a favourite haunt of the Marquis de Sade, himself decidely *cochon*.

Once at Atac, I tentatively presented my abbreviated advert to the girl at the desk. 'Prof. de nat. angl. dipl. d'Oxf. donne cours, tél' was accepted without problem. I pinned it up myself. The board was already very full but I was not unhappy with my eye-catching spot between 'Bargain! Children's tent. As new' and 'Home needed for two Alsatian puppies'. The ad, with its hand-drawn and coloured Union Jack, was quite classy.

Suddenly I was overcome with a terrible doubt. What if my abbreviations weren't correct? The French might read *'professeur de natation anglais donne cours par téléphone'*. I know nothing about swimming. *Tant pis*. Any contact is better than none at all.

I proceeded to do a little shopping – mustard, olive oil, tuna fish, olives – in order to build a reserve in the event of floods, atomic war, flu or lethargy. At the checkout a young girl with a ponytail and a melting smile asked for my *kartatak*. I was flummoxed. What did she mean? Was she talking to me in Inuit? Angélique – as the badge on her nylon Atac smock informed me – explained the *carte Atac* loyalty card system, kindly filled in the application form and – a most exhilarating moment – presented me with the catalogue of gifts to which a faithful patron can aspire. My tin of tuna in virgin olive oil earns me a harvest of 17 points. With a mere 2,400 points I am eligible for three flashing luminous yoyos. An ideal solution for whiling away long winter evenings waiting for the chestnuts to cook on the fire. For an extra 2,500 points I can have four plastic earthenware pots – *des caquelons* – perfect for preparing a nourishing soup which will bring a smile to the faces of the whole family. If I buy a further 394 tins of tuna in virgin olive oil I can have both the yoyos and the *caquelons*.

The clients of the supermarket – *les Ataquants*? – all wore the regulation orange crash helmet, long floppy khaki shorts, acrylic diamond-motif socks and open-toed sandles. In my summer tweeds and well-worn brogues I felt a touch out of place. My new loyalty card gave me my first real sense of belonging.

The second advert was *une autre paire de manches* – another pair of sleeves (or kettle of fish, if you prefer). I drove back through the town and parked on the central square in front of the church. My hands were clammy, the nervousness increased with every moment. I donned my Ray-Bans to preserve my anonymity but as no one knew me it struck me they were probably a good way of drawing attention to myself, so I took them off. The *Maison de la presse* was chock-a-block. As soon as someone left, another person came in – a newspaper, a packet of cigarettes, a postcard, a *morpion. Un morpion?* There was a dictionary on the school shelf. The definition read: 'pubic hair bugs'. Could this be the lice in licentious? Why this sudden run on pubic hair bugs? By studying form I understood. A morpion is a scratchcard. Endless *morpions* succeeded one another. I was never alone. I loitered around the sports magazines. Would I ever pluck up courage?

A cowardly idea dawned. If I were to buy several things at once I should at least be able to *noyer le poisson* – drown the fish, or conceal my intentions. A scratchcard, the local paper *La Nouvelle République*, big enough to hide the other purchase underneath it, and a packet of chewing gum. Back at the house I didn't even bother to scratch my *morpion*. Feverishly I opened the shameful magazine. It was Jean-Pierre Goujon, the butcher of the rue de l'Abbé Grégoire in Paris, who had first spoken to me about *Le Chasseur français*.

The magazine looked innocent enough. On the cover a photograph of a robin perched on a branch, advertising the leading article, 'A tough little bird from northern climes'. But my passion was far from ornithological. I turned to the small ads at the back. To the section 'Contacts', where ladies and gentlemen from all over the

French-speaking world advertised their desires. A middle-aged school teacher from Guadeloupe seeks a companion. A housekeeper from the Mayenne is looking for a man who mustn't weigh more than 100 kilos. A young lady from Angoulême seeks a soulmate who likes rambling and cuddling.

In the course of my first stay in France I had met Edith Delluc, a sophisticated, treacherous, high-flying *parisienne* who performed without a safety net. Edith began my *éducation continentale* before, with elegance and tenderness, dumping me. I often thought of her. She was stored away in a small velvet-lined box in a secret drawer in my heart. On Sundays I would take her out and dust the memory with affection and nostalgia. But memory is not enough.

Having studied style, form, structure, and *double entente* in the pages of *Le Chasseur français*, I had, by the end of the evening, composed a first version of my second ad.

'Assez JH de phys. ag. éd. Ox. aimant poi. ch. JF pour soirée yoyo et caquelon.'

I was none too sure about the abbreviated leek – poi. for *poireaux* seemed unlikely – but evenings of yoyo and earthenware pots did seem to be at once chummy and saucy. Marivaux, the eighteenth-century prince of *libertinage*, would doubtless have approved.

4

Plop.

    Plop?

    Not ... *slurp* or *phew*?

    Odd.

    Plop. There it goes again!

    Just a minute ... it's half-past two. In the middle of the night! I take stock. I am in bed. I am in France. I am in the attic and there are things going *plop* in the dark. In England my unconscious has come to grips with night noises. The cat stretches on the sofa, the dog farts in the rhododendrons, no problem. But I find it difficult to decipher French night noises. The imagination is instinctively alarmist. The fridge purrs, it's a burglar humming. The beam cracks and an intruder in a black cape is tapping on the shutter.

    Plop.

    Where's the light switch? Groping in the void I knock my glass of water over on to the *patois* book.

    '*Palsanquienne!*' (Page 130.)

    Click.

    Plop.

    The floor seems to be covered in small balls of grey wool. As if a cat had been working its claws on the carpet. But there's no cat and no carpet.

    Plop. Another ball of fluff joins the others on the tiled floor.

    A midget astride the main beam is dismantling a

cardigan? Unlikely. Just a minute! Did that ball of fluff move? It did. And another one. Hang on. This is not wool . . .

The floor is littered with minute baby mice. It's raining rodents!

Ugh. Or '*beurk*' as I have learned to exclaim. *Beurk*. How disgusting. Mice don't do this kind of thing in England. English mice watch BBC2 and eat Marmite. They don't jump from beams.

I rub my eyes. Pull yourself together, Sadler. Be sensible. You came to France to enlarge your horizons. This is an enlarging experience. Naked in the middle of the attic surrounded by writhing fluff, I decide to consider my situation positive. Things are fine.

Plop. Another diminutive kamikaze splats on the hard tiled floor.

Naturally very fond of animals, I am overcome with compassion. For many years I have taken great care not to walk on ants since discovering that they have a vocabulary of some 177 words. Words is perhaps not the appropriate term. Ants – or ants with a developed IQ, Mensa ants if you wish – communicate by rubbing their antennae together in different ways at different levels in order to communicate messages such as 'Give me a hand with this crumb'. The same goes for spiders who (please note 'who' and not 'which') I carefully save by transporting them on a lavatory brush from bathroom to garden.

The company of animals has indeed recently been of great comfort. Conversation with humans has been limited to a brief exchange with Eric the feverish plumber and to the same with the charming but evanescent Angélique at Atac. On my second evening I bumped into a mouse in the salon and was very happy to pass the time of day.

'*Bonsoir*, Lucienne.'

'*Bonsoir*, Michael.'

This conversation taking place, it must be said, after a

glass or two of Chinon. Last night I caught Lucienne walking sideways. I subsequently discovered a hole in the lid of the jar of prunes in Armagnac. She was obviously pissed and this made her even more companionable.

My goodness extends itself to bugs. I arrived one very hot September afternoon and found the Velux windows in the attic invaded by a colony of *punaises* bathing in the hot sun. In France, mice booze and bugs tan. Without thinking what I was doing, I reached out for a handy spray and gave them a squirt. I then realised that I had surrendered to some atavistic destructive instinct and was duly horrified. Fortunately, in my distraction, I had mistaken Sophie Hodge's deodorant for a fly spray. Bugs have never smelled better.

Plop.

Something had to be done to forestall the rodent Icarus syndrome.

In the corner of the attic, a spare foam mattress for a single bed. I drag it under the main beam into the flight path of the freefall artists – like a fireman under the windows of a building in flames. Two or three fall immediately, land on the mattress and bounce, emitting a small squeal of pleasure. Mice clearly like trampolining. One problem: the mattress is not big enough to cover the whole landing strip. Far from it. For every two or three trampoliners, there are half a dozen splatchers.

A radical solution leaps to mind: the Hoover in the kitchen cupboard. I heave it upstairs and, on all fours on the floor, unwind the lengthy black cable under the incessant bombardment of the fluff balls.

Plug in. We have suction. Standing naked and on tiptoe in the middle of the bed, keeping a very precarious balance on the soft mattress, I manage to shove the tip of the Hoover behind the main beam. The aim is not to annihilate the mice. My scheme is to suck them up, to carry the machine back downstairs and to rip open the dust bag in

the garden, thereby eliminating the deadly fall and liber-
ating the mice.

In full flight I am overcome by a gnawing worry. What
if my new neighbour Aimé Matou has decided to count
the nocturnal flies buzzing around the rumps of his cows?
If, at this very moment in time, he found himself in the
middle of the field, he could, by raising his eyes to the
lighted window, espy a precariously poised exhibitionist
enacting a scene of unique perversity.

Let us recap. I have just arrived. Aimé first caught me
planting leeks with a pneumatic drill. Fine. Maybe that's
how the English do it. But this! At night they take their
clothes off and prance around naked on the bed waving
a Hoover above their heads. The reputation of my country
is at stake.

I begin to doubt. What if the suck is too strong? The
machine has a dust/crumbs/liquid selector. But no mouse
button. I give up. After a half-hearted attempt at artificial
respiration on one or two of the walking wounded, I
decide to desert the battlefield and move downstairs – not
before having scattered my complete wardrobe across the
floor in order to soften the fall.

The eco-system will have to do without me.

5

Hidden away in the back of the barn I came across an antiquated Rotovator. New-found energy flowed through my system. Maybe I had at last stumbled on the solution to the cement garden?

Now I may not be the world's greatest handyman but I am, at heart, a practical person. I poured some petrol into the rusty tank and pulled viciously on the starting mechanism. Nothing happened. I could have flooded the plugs. With the measured gestures of a skilled mechanic I unscrewed the plug (twenty-three minutes), scratched it with sandpaper (twelve minutes) and then screwed it back in again (six minutes). I then tried again, adding even more gusto to my pulling. Nothing doing. Not to be disheartened, I withdrew some three yards and ran towards the machine giving it an almighty kick in the balls as I uttered the bloodcurling cry of the medieval mechanic: '*Testiguienne!*' (Page 72: mechanical failures.)

The machine still refused to spark into life.

Having now exhausted the totality of my practical knowledge, I gave up and had a drink. At such moments one becomes only too aware of the solitude of country life. In Paris, in the rue de l'Abbé Grégoire, I could have popped downstairs to the Balto to ask Dédé l'Asperge for help. True, he would have been surprised to learn that I was trying to start a Rotovator in my sixth-floor flat, but he would doubtless have dispensed sympathy and wisdom. In the middle of the fields, miles from anywhere, you have only yourself to count on. It's most frustrating.

At that precise moment I spotted Aimé Matou in the neighbouring field, lurking behind the rump of a handy cow. Given his relationship with the Hodges he would probably not be disposed to help, but too bad, I was up to my arse in alligators. I had to speak to him. Easier said than done. In a town you can pretend to bump into someone. You just wait for them to turn a corner:

'*Tiens! Jean-Pierre.*'

'*Tiens! Mike.*'

Et Robert est votre oncle. The countryside, however, is devoid of corners. You can see everyone for miles. Hedgerows would help, but hedgerows are now – since *le remembrement* – few and far between. Indeed, you often come across birds desperate for somewhere to sit down.

Aimé is in his field some hundred yards from the bottom of the vegetable garden. To reach him I am obliged to hew my way through the Amazonian undergrowth. He's not looking in my direction – this would be too manifest a sign of interest – but the general scuttling of rabbits, pythons and other assorted anteaters is doubtless a sign of an approaching *rosbif*. After the jungle, the wheat field. In order not to squash the young shoots I carefully step over them, which means that I have to lift my legs high in the air with every step, looking like Monsieur Hulot wading through a paddy field. Next hurdle, the electric fence. Either I crawl underneath – *Full Metal Jacket*-style – a shade excessive for someone wearing a tweed jacket – or I step over it, running the risk of compromising my desire to found a large family. Only twenty-five metres to go.

Twenty-five metres: peanuts? No sir. The final approach is the trickiest moment. What's the natural thing to do? Do you smile? If so, when? And for how long? Raise a hand? If so, how high? Have you ever tried to cross a bumpy field with one hand in the air and a fixed smile on your lips? And precisely when do you break the silence? And what do you say? 'Aimé!' might sound overweeningly friendly. 'Aimé! At last!' would be too emotional. '*Bonjour*' is more appropriate. But with what degree of enthusiasm? Peasant etiquette is complex.

Aimé pays no attention to me whatsoever. Maybe he is preparing himself for a pastoral version of the urban bump? He probably wants me to surprise him. Which I am about to do and would have succeeded in doing had I not at that precise moment walked *schplatt* into a fresh pile of cowshit. The herd pisses itself laughing.

'*Bonjour*,' I say, using the field as a doormat. Aimé turns his head some 20 degrees west and nods imperceptibly. Obviously a minimalist.

'*Je suis Monsieur Sadler.*'

Another nod.

'I am the Hodges' lodger.'

In fact I said 'I am the Lodges' Hodger'. This made little difference as Aimé clearly preferred the conversation to be in the vernacular. But as I ventured the information I made a mistake. I winked. This wink was meant to convey that I knew that he had once been the Hodges' gardener, that there had been some argy-bargy and that – wink – I was aware that relations were not as friendly as one might have hoped. This is a lot to ask for from a wink. Aimé immediately misread the sign, clearly took it to be a confirmation of what he had already suspected – that the English are a nation of pederasts – and duly retired behind his rump, taking care to lower the cow's tail as he did so (one never knows). I started again.

'*Je viens de repiquer les poireaux.*'

I thought he might reply with something jocular along the lines of: 'Are you taking me for a blockhead? I witnessed your eccentric antics with the pneumatic drill.' Nothing of the kind. Aimé simply nodded again and uttered an extremely elliptical: '*Ça se peut bien.*'

Ça se peut bien? This reply left me temporarily flummoxed. *Ça se peut bien* means 'That may be the case'. This insinuates:

1. That he doesn't believe me.
2. That I don't know what I'm talking about.

Then I remembered my Grandval. Chapter 16: 'Advanced Peasant French'. *La litote paysanne* – bucolic understatement. You say little in order to say much. For instance you say '*bonjour*' when what you really mean is 'arsehole'. Everything needs translating. It's a difficult art. *Ça se peut bien*, in the light of Grandval, seems to mean 'Leeks will never grow in that concrete jungle you tea-drinking lunatic'.

I had a bash at understatement myself.

'*Y a du boulot.*' There's a lot to do.

Which I hoped he would interpret as: 'You've seen the state of the garden. Give us a hand. *Merde!*' With his right hand Aimé pushed the back of his cap so that the peak fell down over his eyes.

'*La terre est basse.*' (Literally: 'The earth is low down'; in translation: 'Get your finger out, *rosbif*!')

And he spits, a rhetorical flourish employed to underline the piquancy of his observation. I reply in the same minimalist fashion.

'*La terre est bien basse.*' (Trans: 'I don't know how to start.') Adding what I hope is a baroque vernacular adornment:

'*Morguienne!*'

And in turn, not to be beaten, I also spit. Unfortunately it has been a long time since I last spat, and the direction of the breeze means that the expectoration lands on the lapel of my jacket. Aimé appears enchanted by the lively exchange:

'*Elle est bien basse.*' (Trans: 'Too bad for you, fatface.')

And I, delighted that the conversation seems to have hit a major theme:

'*Pour être basse elle est basse.*' (Trans: 'Please, Aimé, don't be a shit.')

And he, as sharp as a nail:

'*Pardi.*' (Trans: 'Go take a running jump.')

My back to the wall, I throw ambiguity to the winds.

'*Et très difficile à travailler.*' Very difficult to work.

Aimé had watched me toiling; he knew a beaten man when he saw one. He eyes me with the disdain of Clint Eastwood about to shoot a fly off his spurs:

'*Ça se peut bien.*'

And we're back to square one. The session is closed, the Friesian farts and Aimé moves down two rumps. Enough badinage, there's work to be done.

Reinvigorated by this witty exchange, it was with a light foot that I began the journey back to the vegetable garden. Things are at least clear. Aimé is going to do bugger-all to help me. He's only too delighted to see me flounder and sink, and the Hodges with me. Another front must be opened. It is time to attack the Toison d'Or.

Leaving the car on the decorative pink gravel in front of the church – for once empty of the *Toisonnettes* in their crash helmets – I made my way to the café, passing by the bakery. I bought a large crusty two-kilo loaf from a charming grandmother who served me behind the counter leaning on her Zimmer frame. She had a wicked twinkle in her eye. She looked like the village gossip. I decided to make use of her talents.

'*Bonjour, madame.* I am the new *locataire* of Monsieur *et* Madame Hodge.'

With the gusto which characterises the British when they are embarrassed, I declaimed my CV, explaining who I was, where I came from, where I was going and who was going with me. I took care to intimate that I was no mere passing tourist, whose whim had been tickled by reading this book or that book telling tales of the English settling abroad. No. I was a bona fide traveller, keen to make meaningful contact with *la France profonde*; indeed, if this could be considered within the realms of possibility, to transmogrify myself into a *paysan*.

I had reached the lyrical end to Act One – the exposition – and was about to embark upon Act Two – dramatic development and scherzo – when I became aware that my voice, in a crackly, distorted form, seemed to be coming back at me from the depths of her black and blue flower-print dress. Indeed, my amplified monologue was being broadcast throughout the village from a loudspeaker concealed in her left armpit. It all became clear. Madame Roubaud's antediluvian hearing apparatus had, by some audio fluke, ceased to receive and started to emit. I took note. If ever in the coming months I have a public announcement to make, I shall use Madame Roubaud as a megaphone.

Bread carried ostentatiously under the arm – a sign that I shop in the village – I plucked up courage and opened the door of the café. The inside was dark. A wooden-faced zinc-topped bar on which a few bottles were lined up ready to shoot – Pastis, Ricard 51, Guignolet. The tables and benches were in the same dark wood. On the walls faded calendars of the Union Sportive de Toison. The flowers were plastic and dusty. Deep breath.

'*Messieurs! Bonsouère.*'

Two comments. First, the 'bonsoir' is *de rigueur* in Touraine after midday. Second, Grandval page 12 authenticates the phonological shift from *soir* to *souère*. I had practised in the bathroom before venturing out. I had another bash in case the first was unrecognisable.

'*Bonsouère.*'

The Argonauts – six walruses seated hunched around

a table – did not even deign to look up. I recognised Mr Purple, the gentleman who sat outside his house contemplating his nose, and the municipal handyman. The team was completed by a long thin man wearing a blue cap covered in flour – he must be the baker – a squat toad of a man with a bushy moustache who kept massaging his legs as if he had problems with varicose veins and a shrimp with a stutter whom everyone called – if my hearing was correct – Penthouse.

I was struck with terrible stage fright. These men, their personalities, their legends, belonged to the village. Their parents and grandparents were buried in the cemetery under the big yew tree. I was a mere extra in a pageant that had been played out in Toison for centuries. How could I best make my entry? A cunning ruse dawned in my mind.

I opened my jacket, took out my wallet, fumbled around and ostensibly dropped my Atac card on to the floor at the same time as I uttered: 'Oh!'

Total failure. No one looked up. Either they couldn't give a fart or they were Super U. Sadler 0, Argonauts 1.

Entering a pub in England is another pair of sleeves, as we now have it. In Abesbury everyone around the bar would say a cheery hello/nice day/afternoon/evening, etc. No one listens to what you say or even to what they're saying themselves: the important thing is to be chummy. Even the dogs are pleasant. Not so in Toison. The immediate preoccupation of the Argonauts did not seem to be welcoming. Odd. It can't be every day that an affable *rosbif* pops in to drop his loyalty card on the floor. A whole host of questions must be queueing up. Man or mouse? *Cocu* or not *cocu*? Balls or no balls? But latent curiosity did not even cause a ripple on the surface.

A lady in slippers came from behind the bar to take my order. I was going to ask for a pastis – carefully avoiding the kind of drink such as iced tea that might give the

impression I was a drip. But a second ruse leapt to my
mind. I ordered a mix of extract of gentian and black-
currant liqueur.

'*Une suze cassis.*'

And, once the drink arrived, I triumphantly lifted my
glass and addressed the assembled company.

'*Ça ne suze cassis!*'

I was very proud of this French pun. It was given to
me by Dédé l'Asperge, the pillar of my Parisian haunt, the
Balto. *Ça ne s'use qu'assis*: it only gets worn out by sitting
down. I had rehearsed it in front of the bathroom mirror
but had never used it in public. In private it was a hoot.
Not so in the Toison d'Or. Six pairs of eyes turned and
stared at me as if I had escaped from a lunatic asylum.
Who's the guy with Parkinson's telling bad jokes?

Sadler 0, Argonauts 2.

The possibility of seeking advice about the garden faded.
I decided to pipe down and to listen to their conversation
– an excellent way of tuning into country affairs. I was
excited. This was a long way from *The Archers*. This was
the ancestral *France profonde* I had so often dreamed
about. Their accent was difficult to decipher. I had to listen
very attentively. They looked discontented. What was
wrong? Were they plotting a revolt? Planning to build a
barrage of cauliflowers? To entomb poor innocent British
tourists behind a wall of artichokes? Penthouse put his
hand in his pocket and placed an object on the table. I
had to peer to get a glance. What was it? A ball-bearing
from a combine harvester? A sick carrot? A mole he caught
red-handed in the corn? I squinted through my fingers to
conceal the direction of my gaze.

Odd. It looked very much like a new Nokia 5023. Mr
Purple picked it up like King Kong empalming the fragile
blonde in her satin dress. He dialled.

'*Ren!*'

I presumed he meant '*Rien*' – nothing. He gave it back

to Penthouse who stood up and tried dialling from behind the bar, standing on a table, in the loo, under the green rubber plant.

'*Ren.*'

'*Ren?*'

'*Ren.*'

I took note. *Ren*, not *rien*. It is obviously chic in the country not to pronounce the 'i'. *Ren dans les poches*. Nothing in my pocket. *Ren à faire*. Nothing to do.

'*Ils nous prennent vraiment pour des cons.*'

And as if to prove the extent to which 'they' take them for cretins/fools/idiots, he turns to me. At last: recognition.

'*Pas de réseau.*' No coverage.

'*Vous trouvez ça normal, vous?*'

Of course I didn't find it normal.

'*C'est un complot.*' It's a plot.

'*C'est exprès.*' They do it on purpose.

'*Devine où ça marche.*'

I couldn't guess where it might work. But they were going to tell me. Apparently the three big mobile operators – Bouygues, Itinéris and SFR, doubtless with the zest of Orange – had, no doubt with the help of bribes, commissions, under-the-table payments and suitcases of banknotes delivered by blindfolded chauffeurs, assured that the only place mobile phones will work in the whole canton of Ligueil is in the Atac car park.

'*Ils ne sont pas cons!*'

The complex macro-economic preoccupations of my new-found friends from the Toison d'Or meant that my own horticultural interrogations faded into insignificance.

The vegetables would just have to wait.

6

With the help of a bottle of Chinon I recently composed the following poem in French – my first. It is called *'Sur la beauté des villes'* ('On the Beauty of Towns'). It goes something like this:

> *Ligueil?*
> *Mon œil!*
> *Mais Loches...*
> *C'est* posh.

I am ready to admit that *'mon œil'* – 'pull the other one' – is unnecessarily disparaging and that the bilingual Loches rhyme, although of some sociological acuity, is on the weak side. Hugo would have done a better job. Understandably. In exile on Guernsey he didn't have the local market to distract him.

On market days in Loches I lose control. My gastronomic education had been fashioned by fluorescent peas, Bisto, overcooked chops and custard. Loches was a garden of temptation. Wicker baskets of fresh vegetables still warm from the ground, their cheeks glistening with dew, pigeons, guinea fowl, honey, *foie gras*, turbot, skate, oysters from Cancale, oysters from Paimpol, oysters from St Vaast, flat ones, deep ones, some as big as your head, plump lettuces, vast twenty-kilo truckles of Cantal, *saucissons*, melons, spit-roasted chickens, croissants, *babas au rhum* ... I wanted the lot. All of it. Now. For years I had been

deprived. For years at school I had lived on a diet of
gorilla's armpit and tapioca. Now all this was for me. It
was my due. My reward. I was making up for lost time.
So let's have another spoonful, another slice, another
helping, another dollop.

The town was equally mouthwatering: moats, naves,
transepts, friezes, towers, turrets, palaces, cloisters, crenel-
lations, dungeons, corbels, machicolations and flourishes
of every water. But, however delicious the architectural
menu, each time you lifted your head to admire beauty,
the nostrils were attacked by the promise of more immediate pleasures. I always left for the market with a strict
list: a steak, some green beans, a lettuce, a bottle of Evian
and that's it. Today I bought six melons (a special offer),
a kilo of young turnips, three kilos of charlotte potatoes,
some yellow courgettes, two *andouillettes*, a *jambonneau*,
three bunches of radishes, four lettuces, two cabbages and
a bunch of chard. The next market is not until Saturday.
That's a lot for three days.

Like a squirrel with bulimia, I stowed the hoard in
the boot of the Mazda and started off home. At the
Place de la Préfecture the trouble began. The light turned
red and I stopped to allow a young mother to cross. She
was pushing a mountain pram – specially designed for
taking baby for a walk in rainforests or for Sunday afternoon jaunts in the Himalayas. She was wearing a short,
shiny anorak, tight trousers and extremely chic ankle
boots.

Ping!

The hatchback of the Mazda popped open. Odd.

Was the catch loose? Did it need adjustment? As red as
my car, I got out to close it. Too late. The young mother
and her progeny, also wrapped up in shiny boots and
anorak, were staring with overt disgust at the unspeak-
able contents of the boot. Here I have to come clean.

I had bought a squid. To be precise, I had bought a

practice pack. An average mature squid weighs some ten kilos. This complete unabridged version would doubtless prove too much for a novice. So I had bought five tentacles and a small chunk of the central control unit. For a long time I have cherished a book bought in Italy: *36 Ways of Cooking Squid*. Until Loches my interest had been purely academic, as the grocer in Abesbury was conspicuously low in supplies of cephalopods.

'Dylan!'

The young mother called out to her child, whose bleak, pale face was sinking horrified into the depths of his 15-tog duckdown jacket. One can sympathise. This was Dylan's first contact with the horror of the world. After nine months spent tucked up in the warm ... *Ping!* ... you are suddenly exposed to a squid-kit oozing out of the boot of a red Mazda.

On making my purchase I had said, '*Je voudrais une poulpe.*'

And the rather pretty fish lady corrected me, '*Non, monsieur. Un poulpe.*' We had a little laugh. I lifted up a tentacle to have a quick peek but couldn't for the life of me see anything that might even remotely sex the mass of squidge. The exchange left me embarrassed and I omitted to ask for him or her or it to be slipped into a Tupperware plastic box, and it was handed to me in a run-of-the-mill plastic bag. In the time it takes to drive from the car park under the castle walls to the Place de la Préfecture the little devil had not been twiddling its thumbs. Like some deep-sea Houdini, it had managed to undo the knot in the plastic bag and wriggle free. When the hatchback door pinged skywards it was poised and ready to make its escape. Two tentacles grabbed hold of the bumper ready to use it as a launching pad for a leap to freedom.

Taken aback as I was by the expression of horror on the face of the mother in the tight trousers I had sadly not noticed the precise location of the tentacles. A terrible mistake. When I slammed the boot down, it bounced hard on the squid's fingers.

Two observations:

1. The squid has a non-existent nervous system. You can bite a squid, you can tickle a squid, but it will not respond. Play Wagner to a squid, it will never yawn. The squid is impassive. My squid did not, therefore, suffer.
2. Squids are tough. In Greece cooks go down to the beach to throw them against the rocks in order to soften them up. But it is doubtless true that a beautiful young pagan youth on the Adriatic shore is more attractive to behold than an embarrassed Englishman in Loches, who is substituting the hatchback door of a small Japanese saloon car for the rocks of Piraeus.

If proof of the squid's resistance were needed, the boot didn't close, it simply bounced up again, and the slimy beast edged further forward. Dylan was about to pass out. I stuffed the squid back into the plastic bag and pushed the lot to the back of the boot, planting the jack – no easy feat – on top of the viscous packet. I did then at last manage to close the boot. Too late. The damage to Dylan's psyche has been done. In later life, when he learns to speak, he will be able to tell his father of this appalling meeting with what Jean-Paul Sartre referred to as *La Nausée*.

Beep beep.

An attractive brunette in a Citroën Picasso wanted to get by. I leapt back into the car, after giving Dylan's mum a fleeting apologetic smile which said 'I'm so sorry that I've confronted your son with existential horror', and started up. Back at the house I wedged the squid at the bottom of the freezer and locked the lid.

The hatchback, however, remains a problem. Yesterday at the traffic lights in Manthelan the young girl with tight jeans and a chignon who serves in the café crossed the road in front of me.

Ping!

Strange. Could it be that the car has in some way become a barometer of my libido? How embarrassing. Just imagine. I drive up the Avenue George V in Paris past the Crazy Horse Saloon and the lights flash, the washers squirt and the roof opens. Having no desire to drive about this tranquil pastoral setting behind the wheel of a car which resembles a ladybird on heat, I arranged a rendezvous at the Dumas garage.

Squid erat demonstrandum.

7

An old, damp-stained copy of the gardening magazine *Rustica* found lining a drawer in the kitchen table offered a possible solution to the cement garden headache. The earth must be thoroughly watered in the evening. In the morning the patch will have been softened up and become workable. This is known as the 'constipation principle'. I gave it a try.

Digging is a deeply atavistic activity. When you sink the fork into the earth you rediscover a primitive, long-forgotten rhythm. The thought is vertiginous. Since the beginning of time man has tilled the soil and here you are tilling as one has always tilled, taking one's humble place in a long line of tillers. The technique seems pretty straight-forward. You push the fork into the ground, you lever up the clod and then you push down on the pronged sod with your booted foot to release the twenty-odd kilos of solid mud from the teeth as if you were releasing chunks of grilled pork from a kebab. At least that's the idea.

The slugs chuckle behind me. If you've never heard a slug chuckle, come to Touraine. The de-pronged soddened clod, once glued to the fork, is now glued to the boot. You now use the fork to free it from the boot. It sticks to the fork. You use the boot to free it from the fork, it sticks to the boot. The slugs are by now beside themselves.

I decided to ignore the impaled clod and to carry on digging. A foolish idea. The initial clod (a) simply compresses itself between the prongs to make place for the new clod (b). The instrument becomes impossible to lever because it now weighs (a) + (b) = 50 kilos. A very strong and desperate gardener could in this manner carry on compressing and end up with the whole garden jammed up his fork. In which case he might consider concreting over the resultant hole and painting it green.

Logic was called for. I attempted to regain the path. Easier said than done. With each step my Wellingtons snowballed another lump which compressed, according to the fork formula, the preceding clod. By the time you reach terra firma you can hardly walk on account of having some 200 kilos stuck to your boots. This sticky soil is referred to in Touraine as *la terre amoureuse* – because it clings lovingly. Whatever you do, do not contemplate your lexical acquisitions too long. If the sun dries the mud, you will be stuck to your plinth like a Rodin statue and will have to call the fire brigade.

A pain between thumb and index. My first blister. I was moved by the first stigmata of physical toil. A plaster was called for, the only problem being that the first-aid box was in the bathroom and to get to the bathroom I'd have to remove my boots. The boot remover was on the far side of the kitchen where I had left it under the sink. I managed to extract my foot from one boot by jamming the other boot against the heel. The second boot was more difficult. I was obliged to use my liberated foot as a lever which meant that the twenty kilos of mud were now stuck to the sock.

The phone rang. The phone had never rung before – apart from one or two wrong numbers from an elderly gentleman looking for a certain Georgette. I crossed the kitchen on my heels, heart beating fast.

'*Monsieur Sadler?*'

The voice was soft, quiet, almost evanescent.

'*C'est lui-même.*'

I was rather pleased that I could come up with the

correct reply even when unbalanced by a clod-enhanced sock.

'I saw ze advertisment in Atac. I am interesting in your classes.'

A pupil! *Enfin!*

'When could we make contact? As soon as this afternoon even perhaps?'

'*Avec plaisir!*'

I felt a little idiotic for having replied in French. I must control my emotions. The blister was immediately forgotten. I took a shower, shaved, gave myself a squirt of Malcolm Hodge's *eau de toilette*. The bathroom was immediately filled with the smell of old mole and I was obliged to take a second shower.

The instructions were straightforward. In order to find La Ferme des Rives, which is situated a couple of kilometres from the centre of Toison, you simply follow the signs indicating '*Fromages de chèvres*'. I was very excited at the prospect of approaching the closely guarded secrets of the magnificent goats' cheeses of the Loire Valley – the Sainte-Maures, the Valençays, the Selles sur Cher. I could just imagine the farm, with its tiled roofs tucked away in a green valley surrounded by woods and orchards.

As I approached the farm I was, however, obliged to observe that the countryside was pretty bare. The trees were stripped of their bark and the fields bald, as if they'd been napalmed. I didn't have time to ask questions, however, as the goats – who turned out to be an extremely friendly bunch – came out to greet me. You open the door and they get in the car. You get out and they eat your shoes. You get back in again and there's already one nibbling the gear lever. I even saw one with a packet of cigarettes and another eating yesterday's *Le Monde*. The farmyard was also bare, headless geraniums, headless flower beds, naked bushes, leaveless trees. The herd was clearly peckish.

An attractive young woman, tall, distinguished, pale, an aquiline nose, a pre-Raphaelite satin ribbon in her auburn hair, bids me welcome and introduces herself.

'Florence Mabillon.'

Two fawning goats, clearly jealous of the tenor of their mistress's greeting, set about eating my trousers.

'*Les chèvres!*'

She is imperious.

'Enough! *Assez! Ouste!*'

And the pair lumber off, sulking, like two courtiers ticked off by the Queen.

'Please come.'

The goats, who are clearly bilingual, take the invitation as their own, flash a toothy smile and trip up the steps into the front room.

'*J'ai dit. Ouste!*'

Tails between their legs, they reverse out. Inside, the front room is oddly dark. Florence beckons for me to sit down on a large comfy sofa on which two other goats are watching a quiz show called *Questions pour un champion* on television.

'Life is impossible, Monsieur Sadler.'

She claps her hands. A gaggle of goats who had been squatting on the window-sills jump down into the court-yard and the room is once again bathed in daylight.

'Goats suck.'

I am taken aback by the expression of disgust, which is somewhat out of tune with the Victorian heroine who uttered it. In order to lend the conversation a more posi-tive flavour I begin to sing the praises of the Sainte-Maure and the Valençay. Florence Mabillon interrupts me.

'Cheese is futile.'

The density of this philosophical statement took me by surprise and I was for the moment at a loss to find an argu-ment to defend the ontological pertinency of dairy products.

'*Du thé?*'

A small table has been laid with two delicate china plates, a teapot, and a goat.

'*Ouste! Un morceau de gâteau?*'

'Please. That would be delightful.'

'I am desperate. *Du sucre?*'

Did I hear correctly? Did she say desperate?

'I must escape from this 'ole.'

The teacher intervenes.

'Hole. I must escape from this h-h-h-hole.'

She repeats dutifully.

'I must escape from zis h-h-hole.'

'*This.*'

'Zis. Life in ze country is a suicide.'

'I think we would be more likely to say, "Life in the country leads me to contemplate suicide."'

I begin to feel like a Samaritan giving English lessons.

'*Avec du citron?*'

I would like some lemon, yes. Odd. Florence Mabillon is normal in French and tragic in English. Her sister, married to a businessman, lives in London.

'I would like to live in London. But I stay in zis 'ole.'

'H-H-H-Hole.'

'I dream of ze town. *J'en rêve.* In the country nozzing happens. Birds. Goats. Weather. Shit.'

'Nothing. No thing.'

'Nozzing 'appens. But ze goat eat ze curtains.'

'Eats.'

Suddenly she hears someone approaching.

'You smell?'

I . . . what?

'You smell ze smell?'

Florence's husband enters.

'*Du thé, chéri?*'

Jean-Luc Mabillon is tall, thin, handsome, wearing an Afghan beret and a beard like that of an Old Testament prophet. He used to be in wallpaper but quit.

'Jean-Luc is an 'undred per cent organic, *n'est-ce pas, chéri?*'

She corrects herself. 'A 'undred. Tell Monsieur Sadler ze story of ze *maïs fourragère.*'

And she disappears into the kitchen.

Jean-Luc, at the same time as he eats the crumbly cake, launches into a prophecy. The key to the future is pasture-land. Two infatuated goats join us for the sermon, drinking in every word. The gist is the following. If Jean-Luc feeds his herd on grass he receives no subsidy. If on the other hand he feeds them on silage, he will receive some 500 euros a hectare. In this way the government creates a dependency on the American grain lobby. In all, a heresy. The goats applaud. Raise a clenched hoof and sing the Internationale.

Jean-Luc has to leave. He is working on a substitute energy source – petrol based on Jerusalem artichokes. It has often struck me that four Englishmen in a Twingo after a lunch of boiled vegetables could certainly fart their way from Pimlico to Piccadilly but I have no time to explore the topic. Florence rejoins me.

'Ow you say *bouc* in English?'

'Billy goat.'

'My husband. 'E wash; 'e shower. 'E put ze aftershave. But 'e stink of *ze bouc.*'

Maybe he should try after-chèvre.

'My only 'ope. Ze TGV.'

If, by a wonderful fluke, the route of the projected TGV line was to pass straight through the front room of La Ferme des Rives they would be expropriated and could buy a flat in the rue Jacob in Paris, where Florence could read Françoise Sagan novels, drink tisane and meet me to tighten her syntax. Before I leave she slips me a little gift – about twenty cheeses in a plastic bag. I want to protest.

'Take ze lot, Mr Sadler. Take ze 'ole bloody lot.'

Jean-Luc also produces organic vegetables. Florence slips

me a bunch of atrophied radishes and a neurotic-looking cauliflower. As she does so, the evening sun sets fire to her cascade of auburn hair. But the herd gives us no chance of a moment alone. When I get back into the car they throng around me with their devilish grins.

'*Au revoir, professeur . . .*'

And they lift a mocking cloven hoof to wave farewell.

Once back at the house, I go down to inspect the experiment. The clods and sods of the vegetable garden have dried out in the afternoon sun. I am now faced with an expanse of hard little dumplings.

How the hell can I sow seeds in field of dumplings?

8

To repair the hatchback of the Mazda I booked it in at the garage of Monsieur Dumas on the road between Toison and Mouzay.

In an English garage the scenario would be as follows: you arrive in the spotless reception area, all rubber plants and posters of Fangio on the wall, where a receptionist with a white coat and a degree fills in the form on his computer and dispatches the printout via a mechanic with five A-levels and a jumpsuit to the shop floor where a foreman with twenty-five years of experience and a vast salary hands it to an apprentice who fetches the nut on a shelf in a warehouse designed by an award-winning Finnish architect. This impeccable service will cost you £35 an hour plus the price of the nut which is generally 6p.

Things are different in Touraine. The courtyard of the Dumas garage is like a set for a post-Holocaust drama – a tractor has collided with a washing machine, a spindrier with a Peugeot, and they're all piled one on top of the other in a rusty heap. The whole place is an archeologist's paradise. The first layers contain the debris of the consumer society: Polish freezers, Estonian Hoovers, Lithuanian hairdriers, all guaranteed non-repairable. Behind them the remains of the first industrial era: small pink tractors with vertical exhaust pipes, complete with a driver's seat which looks like an upside-down colander.

Digging even deeper you come across remains of the
war: bits of tanks, shrapnel, the spare wheel of a jeep, a
sign indicating the frontier between Free France and the
Occupied Zone. With time, and a few weeks of patient
toil, one would doubtless uncover yokes, harnesses, and
paraphernalia for ploughing with oxen. A long way
from Renault Croydon.

'Monsieur Dumas.'

Monsieur Dumas' chubby legs were sticking out from
under the carcass of an elderly orange Renault 12.
Monsieur Dumas is to be seen every Monday morning
at the market in Ligueil walking a few steps behind his
imposing and more colourful wife. He is in his fifties,
plump and squat as a leek, always dressed in a beige
garbardine jacket zipped over a tartan scarf. He wears
mole-coloured suede boots, a two-tone brown diamond-
pattern pullover, a shiny semi-see-through shirt, and a
thin black belt which is unnecessary as his paunch keeps
the Terylene trousers firmly in place. For the regular
Friday evening visit to La Vie Auchan, the big hypermarket on the outskirts of Tours, he takes his black
leather handbag – a present from his daughter-in-law
for Father's Day – and wears a tartan cap with a
pompom.

'*Monsieur l'Anglais!*'

Monsieur Dumas belongs to that generation for whom
a foreigner is still an exotic entity.

Nimble for a man of his build, he exited from under
the Renault on his elbows. I explained the problem with
the volatile hatchback without going into my sexual
proclivities. Monsieur Dumas winked. No problem. He's
going to put a sign outside the garage: *Clientèle internationale!* This calls for a celebration.

'*Vous prendriez bien un petit verre?*'

The Dumas residence, like so many new houses in the
Indre et Loire, is perched on a small artificial hillock.

In Turkey they create dwellings by excavating cliffs; in Thailand everything is on stilts; in France the traveller encounters the hillock syndrome, endless houses posed on top of a hump. This is the Napoleon complex. Ever since Austerlitz the French have liked to take their *café croissant* overlooking the battlefield of life.

At the front door we take off our shoes as if we were entering a mosque and put each foot on a thick flannel skate – *un patin* – which we use to navigate the extremely polished and highly slippery wooden floor.

'*Thérèse!*'

I was sinking into a vast studded imitation leather armchair bought at a knockdown price during the buffalo hide week at La Maison du Meuble when Madame Dumas made her entry, skating in from the kitchen. I pushed down on the arms of the chair to stand up but misjudged the weight distribution and the chair slid rapidly backwards behind me while my feet, still resting on the flannel skates, shot forward. I was now virtually horizontal. Monsieur Dumas pirouetted and deftly pushed the armchair back under my posterior while Madame Dumas blocked my feet, preventing them from slipping even further forward. This all appeared to be quite normal. A pre-dinner drink in Toison is an acrobatic business.

My host skated over to a glass-fronted cabinet which he opened to unveil his vast collection of apéritifs. Here were all those names I had long eyed over the counters of endless bars: Ambassadeur, Guignolet, Suze, Cinzano, Americano, Byrrh, Amer Picon, Avèze-Gentiane, Dubonnet, Campari, Banyuls, Pineau, Saint-Raphael, Noilly Prat, Rivesaltes, Bartissol, Madère, Porto Cruze, Beaumes-de-Venise . . .

'*Alors?*'

While I was attempting to make my choice, Madame Dumas set about emptying packets of nibbles into a huge tray, tearing the corner of the packet with her specially designed teeth. Today's menu included the famous Monster Munchies, Peppi's with their original salty tang, Crunchips Stackers, salmon-flavoured Topaki, Feuilltey's with their classy apostrophe, Shuttles, Crackers Télé, Triangolinis, Big Bang Chipsters, Dixi tomato crunch, chorizo-flavoured Papyrus, Fritelles, Curlies, and finally the cheesy Astro rigolo. The Dumas are clearly professionals – *des pros de l'apéro*. My favourite? The irresistible Cheeto's Fantom – a cheese biscuit in the form of a ghost, tasting like crispy ectoplasm.

It was beginning to rain outside and Monsieur Dumas suggested that, as this was perfect weather for a tasting, we would start on the left and work our way along the shelf in alphabetical order beginning with Amer Picon. I tried to protest.

'*Non, vraiment*. Just a drop . . . *Une larme*.'

Une larme, a mere tear? You're joking. The Dumas were French without tears. My body quickly underwent a series of physiological changes. The first sensation was one of pleasure. Taste filled the mouth as if an abundant ladle full of summer fruit had been slipped down my willing and waiting throat. After the third apéritif taste was transformed into heat, and the flames of hell began to burn. This inner blaze first coloured the nape of my neck and then, with the rapidity of a Corsican bushfire, began to inflame cheeks and nose. The *rosbif* is now on fire. And once alight he's very difficult to extinguish. The eyes are glazed, the skin becomes marbled and blotchy. Observe the British apéritif drinker. If at the time of the sixth apéritif his fingers start groping in his glass for an ice cube, he is looking for a handy extinguisher to slip down the neck of the shirt in order to douse the fire.

'*Encore un* . . .'

'*Mais non . . .*'
'*Allez. Quand même . . .*'

Vision becomes blurred. Spectacles mist over – only you're not wearing spectacles. You are now approaching the final stage. Between apéritif eight and ten you begin to kiss everyone around you – host, hostess, handy children, dogs, gerbils, anything that comes to hand – all the while expressing a deep love for mankind and singing the 'Marseillaise'. In a word, you are pissed.

I'd been holding back for too long. I just had to tell the Dumas the truth about my boot. I arrived at the lights – *aux feux de la Pleflectoure. Non, la proficture – non . . .* The attractive mother in her shiny anorak crosses the road and – *ping!* – up pops my boot. And there in the boot . . . *mon poulpe!* The Dumas are hysterical. Heedless of danger we stand on our felt skates. Madame Dumas plays the tarty young mother, I do the squid and Monsieur Dumas does the hatchback door.

Ping!

What an evening. This is what I call an apéritif. We can't keep our balance but we don't give a fart. Like a trio of acrobatic Russians, the crowd roaring its support, we skate out into the middle of the arena, perform an arabesque and back again, clinging to the walls for support. For the grand finale Madame Dumas, on her way to replenish the Cheeto's, attempts the triple axle: she throws herself into the air, turns like a corkscrew, I catch her, toss her to Dumas, who flips her over like a crêpe and catches her again! What a performance. The Banyuls flows like water. Heedless of the cost we toss the chipsters into the aquarium. *La vie est belle.*

Ding dong.

The front door chimes brought us back to earth.

Monsieur Dumas recovered his professional aplomb with an ease which astounded me. While Madame

Dumas hoovered up the wayward nibbles and cleaned the fishtank with a small net, Monsieur Dumas went to answer the front door. He returned in a trice, beckoning me to follow him.

The newcomer had parked his Citroën BX in front of the garage doors. Dumas signalled for him to back in. From the boot his friend took out an old television set, an antiquated PC and a washing machine. Dumas was evidently the local Mr Fixit. He must be an ace handy-man. I watched him with respect and attention. He plugged appliances into a large multiple socket in the wall. There was an immediate flash of light and an explosion. Smoke poured out of the machines. The whole garage was full of the smell of burning. I was taken aback. Dumas had fried the circuits!

'*Mais . . .*'

Dumas winks.

'*C'est le 720.*'

Seven hundred and twenty volts!

Dumas winks again.

'*C'est pour l'assurance.*'

Last week there had been a terrible storm, *n'est-ce pas* wink. Most of the electrical appliances of the commune had been struck by lightning, *n'est-ce pas* wink. They'll all have to be changed. *Hein?* The insurance companies will want to inspect, *hein? Alors?* Monsieur Dumas is not only a brilliant mechanic, he is also a high-voltage artist.

I began to feel as if I'd been plugged into the 720 myself. After a quick glass or two with Monsieur Dumas' friend, who had brought along an interesting concoction made from hawthorn roots, *gnôle*, sugar, dragon's gums and Semtex, I made my farewells. Odd. As I left, I noticed Monsieur Dumas' friend looked exactly like him. Same clothes, same build, same zipper jacket, same pompom. Or am I seeing double?

I managed to stumble upstairs for a welcome forty-two-hour nap.

Vive les garages de campagne!

9

The postman is not a *facteur* – *c'est une factrice*! Her name is Laetitia. She has freckles, dimples, a turned-up nose and a smile that makes the cherries blush. When she comes up the drive with her cheeky *bip-bip* I come running.

Letterless days are Laetitialess days. When I see the roof of the little yellow van above the burgeoning corn in Aimé Matou's field I long for her to slow down, to make the turn up the path that leads to the drive. When the van speeds past, my heart falls. I'm not sure what I miss most, the letters or the postwoman. If I want a daily visit from the van I must take steps – *Le Chasseur français* comes out once a month. I need something readable which comes out every day. Even twice a day.

When Laetitia does deliver I use strategies to make sure that her visit – honed down to the last second by the time-and-motion boys at 'La Poste' – lasts as long as possible. To hell with it if Aimé Matou gets sixteen seconds less. Life is a jungle. First I greet her with a hearty *'Bonjour!!!'* followed by a series of exclamation marks in order to manifest my pleasure at seeing her.

'*Vous avez quelque chose pour moi!*'

Of course she's got something for me otherwise she wouldn't be here, but words – especially those spoken in hesitant French – delay.

'*Tiens, une lettre.*'

What was I expecting? Goldfish?

'Now who could this be from?'

This last remark borders on the cretinous. It's extraordinary the effect that dimples can have on an otherwise healthy mind.

I have never been so pleased to receive junk mail. The DIY lorry Outiror from Saint-Etienne will be on the Place du Blé in Ligueil on the thirteenth. Among the attractions on offer: a terracotta squirrel, a farting gnome for your garden ('Surprise your guests!'), a transistorised toilet-roll dispenser (you pull and it plays 'The Flight of the Bumblebee') and a false barometer in which you can hide your front-door keys. From the 14th to the 18th, Intermarché is offering knockdown prices for pork. Home-reared chops smile at you on the front cover for only 8 euros a kilo. If by any chance you've lost your keys you can hide your chops in the barometer. Laetitia's freckled smile as she hands me armfuls of this muck transforms spam into caviar.

Bip-bip

Laetitia!

I was in the garden and had not seen the yellow roof in the corn. Post at last! I run to the top of the drive preparing something charmingly mindless to say.

Bip-bip

I fly, *factrice* of my dreams, I fly.

Bip-bip

Odd. I don't recognise the *bip-bip*. Normally langorous, today it is insistent. The glare of the morning sun reflects on the windscreen, hiding Laetitia from view.

'*Bonjour.*'

'*Bonjour.*'

I immediately withdraw any exclamation marks. Who is this oaf with a peaked cap and a uniform?

'*En vacances?*'

No. I'm not on holiday. What a stupid question.

'*On s'amuse?*'

No, I am not having a good time. I am struggling with

an arable wasteland all the while attempting to foster an idyll with a freckled *factrice*.

'*On prend du bon temps?*'

Is he going to continue asking variants of the same bloody question? Where's Laetitia?

'*Ahahaaa . . .*'

A-ha?

'*Vous aussi?*'

Me as well what?

'*Ils sont tous fada de la Laetitia.*'

'*Fada*': *Le Petit Robert*, p. 125: crazy, mad, obsessed. He continues, imitating me.

'"*Elle est où la Laetitia?*"'

Quite. Where is she?

'*Laetitia était ma remplaçante.*'

Oh no. While this ruddy hulk was in hospital for a check-up, Laetitia took his place. He had a blood-pressure problem: up to 120/200.

Not enough? Apparently far too much. But now unfortunately it's come down to 80/120.

'Bernard's back!'

Merde.

There are ladies, he says with a smile, who are delighted to see Bernard. He hands me my letters and a magazine. Distraught, I look at the cover. I've just taken a six-month subscription to *Stamps International*. Twenty-four euros for six months of Bernard!

Back in the kitchen I kick a few pieces of furniture to vent my frustration. A flier falls to the floor. A handwritten photocopy of a letter from the *mairie* – the local town hall.

CONCOURS DES JARDINS

The annual competition for the best garden will be judged at the fête de Toison to be held this year on the 3rd of September. Those wishing to take part should enrol at the *mairie*. The jury will announce the results of the competition on the place de l'Eglise at six o'clock in the evening on the day of the fête.

The world is transformed. I can see the doting eyes of Laetitia looking up at me in admiration as I am carried shoulder-high in triumph around the village. Bernard is a thing of the past. I slip off my boots and scrub my fingernails to go down to the *mairie*. This is what I needed. You just wait and see, Aimé Matou.

Greenfingers is back in town.

10

The town hall of the village of Toison, a bastion of the *République* standing plum opposite the church, looks like a picture-postcard of deepest France. The compact building is made of white limestone and pink brick. Steps lead up to a small terrace from which speeches can be made, and a vine twists its way around the inscription *Liberté Egalité Fraternité* as if to remind us of what the revolutionary formula omitted to mention – that it is the grape which binds together life's essentials. At the bottom of the steps a flowerbed, in which Pois Chiche, the municipal handyman, in a moment of patriotic botany, planted the colours of the French flag. Unfortunately Pois Chiche bought the petunias in the DIY superstore Castorama at a knockdown price the day after the local booze-up – *la fête des laboureurs* – at which he himself had been knocked down by a particularly persuasive Vouvray. As a result, he was slightly brash in his selection of the bedding plants – merely in bud at the time of the purchase – and the white ones turned out to be yellow. Toison has thus the particular distinction of being the only village in France to display in its municipal flowerbed the flag of Venezuela.

I had a dream.

I'll be elected the first English mayor of Toison. This will give me the privilege of marrying and kissing all the pretty girls from the village, of leading the 14th of July Bastille Day parade, of having the best seats for the annual bike race and of having my place and my *andouillette frites* reserved at the village fête. People will hail me in the street, *'Bonjour, Monsieur le Maire'*, and I'll reply with a discreet nod of the head, not allowing status to swell my ankles (*avoir les chevilles enflées*, to have a big head) but I might be tempted, on special occasions, to wear the mayor's insignia – the red, white and blue Republican scarf – in bed with my pyjamas or, on even more special occasions, without my pyjamas.

The highlight of my term of office would be the twinning of Toison with the picturesque Cotswold village of Abesbury. A 'French day' would be instituted in England and an annual 'English day' in France. Maureen in the local sub-post office would be greeted with a guttural *'Salut, ça gaze Renée?'* While in Toison Aimé Matou in his *bleu de travail* would hail Pierrot, who was on his hands and knees extracting a stone from his 1952 yellow combine harvester, with a jolly 'In a pickle, Peter?' Cricket would be played on the *boulodrome*, *pétanque* on the village green, tisane would be served in the Toison d'Or and *gnôle* at the vicarage.

I opened the door. The mayor turned around, startled. *'Excusez-moi.* I'm a little on edge. A shade jumpy.'

Monsieur Gossard is an ex-military man, his grey hair still cut short in a regimental crewcut. He is *'sans étiquette'*, meaning he was not elected as representing a political party – no label, that is, apart from the one sticking out from the back of his blue pullover recommending a machine wash at 40 degrees. He was in the process of stirring a thick, sticky white concoction in a glass.

'Pour la digestion,' he explained apologetically.

Acid digestion goes with the job. He pointed to a town plan stuck to the wall with *punaises* – bugs, or drawing pins – and covered with Post-it notes. This, he explained, is the new municipal headache. I noticed the dark rings under his eyes. Clearly he was not sleeping too well. He burped. It all began with the postman.

'*C'est Clochemerle, Monsieur Sadler.*'

He offered me a digestion tablet as if the tale itself were sufficient to induce instant acidity. A few years ago the French Post Office, in order to reduce the time it took for the postman to do his round and to diminish the subsequent danger to his liver, decided to rationalise the delivery of letters and to this end grouped the letterboxes in the middle of the village. To each inhabitant his or her grey metal box. This in itself caused problems. Denis, the tightrope walker, only had 50 yards to get to the boxes – in itself a good thing because even on good days it might take him several weeks – whereas Madame Roubaud on her Zimmer frame had to cross some 230 yards. This inequality being deemed unconstitutional, it was resolved that the postman would once again do his rounds in the village but that, in order to speed up the process, the village would have to name its streets.

Gossard turned back to the plan bugged to the wall. All this should be *aussi simple que bonjour*, as simple as falling off a log. Toison is not Bombay. In all there are four streets, the church square and a transversal path which cuts the village in half and which runs past Gilbert Chougras' vegetable garden. Just seven names to be found.

Pas la mer à boire? No big deal? I had another think coming.

Gossard took a dossier from his municipal briefcase. The town council, in its wisdom, had decided to consult the village on the matter. A fatal error. Because the village replied. And the 187 able-bodied voters constituting all the population of Toison had come up with 187 x 7 = 1,307 different suggestions. Somewhat excessive for six streets and a dirt track.

Gossard gave me a few examples: Place Kronenbourg, Avenue Sophie Marceau, Impasse François Mitterrand (conservative voter), Impasse Jacques Chirac (socialist voter), Rue de l'Andouillette, Place Leonid Brezhnev, Place Général de Gaulle, Allée Brigitte Bardot, Avenue Zidane.

What could he do?

Ren, I replied in an authentically Toison-like fashion. *Ren*. This was precisely the problem. The village was at daggers drawn. And being at daggers drawn is what peasants are best at. Age-old grievances had risen swiftly to the surface like so many dead whales. Ancestral splits between Cain and Abel, between the eldest and the youngest, between left and right, the church and the State, the organic farmers and the non-organic farmers, the tall farmers and the short farmers, the Crédit Agricole and the Crédit Lyonnais, between Super U and Atac, between *petit pois fins* and *petit pois extra fins*, between Snuggies and Pampers, any excuse would do for a rift.

Burp.

Gossard was victim of yet another republican spasm. What a terrible job.

On leaving the *mairie* I paused at the top of the steps to address the crowd of three moustachioed ladies in their orange crash helmets waiting patiently for my decision in front of the Venezuelan flag and who appeared to be deeply disappointed when I announced that, after much soul-searching, and with deep regret, I had decided to withdraw from the electoral battle.

11

My ad in Atac has proved rather successful.

I am invited to dinner in Loches by a family of dentists. Madame Tricot has heard tell of my talents (could it be that Florence's goats have been indiscreet?). The Tricot – no plural form for French family names – would be delighted to meet me. To know English in ze modern day iz so important, *n'est-ce pas?*

This invitation was at once flattering and embarrassing. I had a good look at my molars in the cruel neon light of the bathroom. Off-white would be the kindest description. Could it be an overdose of Vouvray? I scratched them with a fingernail, to no avail. Off to the *pharmacie* in Ligueil.

'*Bonjour, monsieur,*' I manage to say with my mouth closed, never having liked confessing my defects in public. If I asked for teeth-whitener, *le tout* Ligueil would immediately twig that the *rosbif* had yellow choppers. To disguise myself would be a little over the top. If I wore a balaclava, I am more likely than not to be arrested ('BRITON IN TOOTHPASTE HOLD-UP'), thereby defeating the purpose of attempting to remain anonymous. I thus determined, as with *Le Chasseur français*, to buy a couple of red herrings – some skin cream and a miracle cure for constipation.

Back at the house, I brushed my teeth three times in quick succession. The yellow did appear a shade less buttercup than before. Unfortunately the result of my dental brass-rubbing was that I splattered the bleach paste all over my black T-shirt. This deposit appeared to be indelible.

The invitation was for Thursday evening. I drove up into the old town, passing through what is called '*la herse*' – the portcullis. Portcullis must surely come from the French – *porte coulissante* – sliding door. So why call it *une herse*? I jot the idea down on a piece of paper in case I need to appear intelligent in between courses. I turn right, up a steep incline bordered with the impressive stone walls of the large medieval town houses, and out on to the tree-lined walk which leads to the park and the dungeon. The other guests have already arrived – an array of Mercedes, Audis and top-of-the-range Peugeots puts the Mazda to shame. I am delighted to see another one hidden behind a tree and park next to it.

The old town is bathed in the rich evening light. Imposing bourgeois domains shut themselves off from the world behind vast, carved, wooden double doors. Concealed behind the wisteria, a bell-pull. I give it a tug to announce my arrival. By mistake I pull on the wisteria and a load of pigeon shit falls in my hair. A quick comb and I start again.

The door is opened by Madame Tricot herself. Ariane is tanned, lithe, with tennis arms, jogger's calves and short, very blonde hair. I can see her strapped into the bucket seat of a flimsy deltaplane, dangling by her harness from a rocky over-hang, or surfing a giant wave wearing nothing but a Brazilian monokini. Tonight she is in Cacharel and – at least I trust – unaware of the fantasies she arouses.

I am ushered into the *salon* and introduced to the other guests, who are all – apart from the director of the local Crédit Agricole – dentists. Their perfect teeth put my British set to shame – they are cast in the Versailles tradition while I am more mixed borders; order and geometry versus exuberance and profusion. I reach for my Ray-Bans to avoid being dazzled.

A specialist with imposing side whiskers and a large whisky begins to bore the knickers of us with a lengthy discourse on the Plantagenets and their contribution to local history. Fortunately he chokes on a peanut in the early fifteenth century and has to dash to the kitchen for a glass of water. Brice, Ariane's husband, seems to be wearing a skirt. I am quick to realise that it is in fact a kilt worn backwards – he is the chairman of the local Scottish association but doesn't seem to know his dirk from his sporran. He passes a plate full of *amuse-gueules* – tempting titbits. I long to tell him that they are too filling but my dentist joke doesn't work in French.

The Crédit Agricole man is very pleased with himself. He bought two cases of Château d'Yquem at the *foire aux vins* in the Leclerc hypermarket and has just sold them for double the price.

'It's not a cellar you've got, Gérard,' says the Plantagenet. 'It's a vault.'

Such wit. We all fall about.

Claude-Henri, the last to arrive, is a *stomato*. At first I thought I heard tomato – but I am a little behind in the conversation and am trying to ketchup. No, a stomato is neither a fruit nor an overweight Japanese wrestler. Claude-Henri is a stomatologist. He is also very pleased with himself. He has bought himself a little present.

'*Je me suis payé une danseuse.*'

A dancing girl?! I am surprised that in the refined quarters of Loches one is unabashed at displaying the knick-knacks brought back from Bangkok. He invites us outside to have a peek. A dancing girl outside on the street! She's going to catch her death of cold.

'*Elle est vieille, mais elle est belle.*'

My heart begins to bleed for the superannuated lapdancer left outside in her thong in the evening breeze.

I am relieved to discover, when the boys – *les garçons* –
are invited outside to try her out, that the acquisition turns
out to be an Italian sports car.

'*Une Maserati.*'

'*Dis donc, dis donc.*'

'*Pas mal. Pas mal du tout.*'

Une danseuse, when I had a chance to look it up, is a
metaphor for an expensive luxury. Being the last to arrive,
Claude-Henri had only found a parking space next to my
own *danseuse*. As they subject the Maserati to close examination, the boys use the Mazda as if it were a sofa. They
lean on it, sit on it, put their whisky glasses on the roof,
use the bonnet like an armchair. Clearly they have never
seen a Mazda before and mistake it for new street furniture installed by the town council.

As they wax ecstatic about Claude-Henri's new toy, I
am struck by their shoes. They all wear sneakers with
tassels – *des glands*. I make a mental note. Last time I was
in the DIY superstore Leroy Merlin, I saw a packet of
curtain tassels. Four gold ones for 1.50 euros. Next time
I'll buy a packet and glue them to my brogues.

A bell rings from deep within the house.

'*On va se taper la cloche.*'

We all fall about again, especially me who doesn't understand a word. To hit the bell. To eat. The bell being the
head; the knife and fork being the clappers. As we troop
inside, Claude-Henri turns for a last loving look at his car
and, never dreaming that the Tricot would ever play host
to a Mazda-owner, remarks that he's unsure he should
leave his *danseuse* in the company of a geisha.

I am introduced to the children – my future pupils. The
boy, who is wearing grey trousers and a blue pullover –
the kind of outfit a congregationalist minister might wear
at a hoedown – looks as if he's in his early fifties. He is
in '*khâgne*', she in '*hippo*'. I daren't ask what this means
for fear of appearing stupid – I am supposed to teach

them, after all – but I'm lost. *Hippo*, to the best of my knowledge, is a meat restaurant on the Boulevard Montparnasse; *khâgne*, at last phonetically, a film festival on the Côte d'Azur. Your guess is as good as mine. *Comprenne qui pourra.**

Hippo is wearing a blue pleated Sunday school skirt to match her brother's pully. She would have loved to do her hair in plaits but her mother stopped her at the last minute for fear she might be taken for Goldilocks in drag. He reads Homer, she rides horses. Maybe that's what 'hippo' means? Ariane is delighted but bewildered.

'When zey come back from school I say darlings, *mes chéris*, come and relax, come and watch something stupid on ze télévision but no . . . All zey want is to work . . .'

The coded conversation starts up again. The son is hesitating between X (I have a quick peek at his flies and for the life of mean can't spot the potential), the Mines (why study Homer to work the coalface?) and HEC, which must, from the look of him, mean 'Hommes Extra Constipés'.† The two children speak English better than I do. What the hell am I going to teach them? Dinner is served. All the guests act delighted when the maid brings in the main course.

'*Miam miam!*' Which is the French for yummy.

Amorosa, the maid, is dark-haired, Portuguese and very popular. Whenever any of them has a dinner party it is always Amorosa who cooks and serves. Amorosa hands me a shell-shaped plate filled with a brownish sauce. At a sign from our hostess we all begin toying with our sauce, as Brice in his skirt does the rounds serving a Korean

---

* Fruits of my research. *Hippokhâgne* and *khâgne* are the names given to the two years you spend slaving away at school after the *baccalauréat* to prepare for the entrance exam to one of the '*grandes écoles*'.

† Three top-flight '*grandes écoles*': 'X' is the distinguished *Ecole Polytechnique*; 'Mines' the *Ecole des mines*, a similar boffin hotbed; and HEC the *Ecole des hautes études commerciales*, a top business school.

Chablis. I was hoping to find some delicious Portuguese salt cod under the brown blanket but everything seems to be suffocated in cornflour. Perhaps Amorosa only cooks dentists' food: soft gunge, neither hard enough to crack a crown nor runny enough to fill a cavity.

The conversation has a similar texture. We begin by talking about a handful of local artists; did you see the last Voloditch exhibition? Two of his paintings are hanging on the wall behind us. A collision between a jam tart and the walls of the old town, and a peony in distress in heavy seas. Does abstract art have a meaning? A meaning maybe not, a price certainly. Both works seem to have been painted using Amorosa's brown gunge.

French cinema provides the next subject for debate. They are all anti. French cinema is subsidised, they don't like it and don't want to pay for it. They much prefer Broussevilisse. Broussevilisse turns out to be Bruce Willis, much fancied by the ladies, while the *garçons* go for Demi-mûre, which I first thought to mean half a blackberry before realising they were referring to the ex-Madame Vilisse. For strategic reasons I open my mouth as little as possible but I do here attempt to join in – speaking of a funny Belgian film I had recently seen about the sex life of the handicapped. This doesn't go down too well with the *garçons*. Anyone who has the slightest interest in Belgian spastics must be either bent or Marxist. The ladies leap to my defence.

With the pudding – a slightly more solid version of Mr Voloditch's splodge period – the gentlemen begin to recall their schoolboy memories. They were all at a private school called St Gatien in Tours. They regale us with side-splittingly funny stories of their old teachers. Ducasse, who walked in the wastepaper basket. *Quel con!* Lentier, who never did his flies up. *Ah, la braguette de Lentier!* And especially Savin, the English teacher, and his famous rhymes they all had to learn off by heart and which, unfortunately, they had never forgotten.

'*Attendez* . . . "What noisy noise annoys a noisy oyster."
C'est ça, non?'

And another one.

'*Vous vous rappelez?* "If Santa supposes his toesies are
rosies, as Santa supposes erroneously."'

The stomato stands and, a glass of Peruvian claret in
hand, declaims:

'Mrs Piper picked a peck of pickled apples . . . A peck
of pickled apples Mrs Piper picked!'

Not to be beaten, Crédit Agricole joins him arm in arm:

'How many chucks could a woodchuck chuck if a woodchuck could chuck wood!'

As a man the dentists then turn to me.

'*Professeur, professeur!* Correct ze pronunciation. You
must! You must!'

And they beat on the table with the back of their spoons.
I reluctantly comply.

'Of course, yes. Well. The "i" in Mrs Piper should be
pronounced as in the French "*paille*", not "Peeper" as in
"peeping tom".'

In order to pronounce clearly I have to open my mouth.
And when I open my mouth I show my teeth. This is Yellow
Peril red alert. Fortunately Ariane comes to my rescue.

'*Les garçons, s'il vous plaît.* We haven't asked poor
Monsieur Sadler here to work!'

Dessert – a gooey tart – follows. The boys choose
between a selection of malt whiskies and the ladies have
a tisane. The Plantagenet threatens to resume his peanut-
interrupted lecture but Ariane saves us, turning down the
lights and proposing one or two amusing slides of their
holidays *en Provence*.

'*Dans le Lubéron*,' adds the stomatologist.

Ariane corrects him. Not the Lubéron. The Luberon.
Luberon without an accent. This clearly makes a big difference and not wanting to be thought unsophisticated or
plouc we all practise getting it right.

'*Lube . . . ron . . . Lube . . . be . . .*'

The first slide is of a crowded Saturday morning market in Apt. Ariane has a little electronic pointer which allows her to move a red arrow over the screen. It picks out a pretty shoulder near a *saucisson* stall.

'Whose? Guess. *Devinez qui.*'

We give in. *Nous donnons notre langue au chat* – we give our tongues to the cat.

'Emmanuelle Béart!'

'*Non! C'est fou!*'

What a famous shoulder. We're all thrilled to bits. Next slide, the crowded marketplace in Le Coustellet on a Sunday morning, and a pensioner disguised as a rock star hiding behind a melon.

'*Devinez!* Guess!'

Silence.

'Johnny Hallyday!'

'*Non!*'

So chic. *La classe!*

'And this.'

A green dustbin? Why take pictures of dustbins?

'*Alors? C'est à qui la poubelle?*'

We scratch our heads. Whose dustbin could it be? Ariane is triumphant.

'*C'est la poubelle de John Malkovich!*'

No! Malko's dustbin! We can't believe our eyes. Wow! Ariane assures us there's no mistake. There follows a series of shots of the aforesaid bin from different angles, including one from the nettles which must have been very painful if Brice was wearing his kilt when he took the snap. There are even a couple of shots of the contents of the bin. John seems to go for apricot yoghurts and *carottes rapées*. The girls are in seventh heaven, excited by this glimpse of the intimate life of the star. Ariane tells us that rumour has it that he even grows his own vegetables.

'*Ce n'est pas possible!*'

'*Il fait son potager!*'
'*C'est tellement sexy!*'
I jump into the breach.
'*Moi aussi.* I grow mine too!'
'*Non!*'
'*Si!*'
Delighted, Ariane, for the first time, pronounces my name in that inimitable fashion which was always to cause an immediate meltdown of my kneecaps.

'*Maï-quel! Maï-quel! C'est vrai?*'
Using the turn I had rehearsed to impress Sophie and Malcolm Hodge, I launch into a new version of the vegetable panegyric (itself very tasty served with mayonnaise). Having succeeded in creating a link between myself and Malkovich, I bask in the ladies' attention. This has the immediate effect of alienating the medical fraternity. Who is this intruder? Joan of Arc was right. Kick the buggers into the sea. The Plantagenet begins to glower at me from behind his whiskers.

He's right to glower. In the warm half-light of a glass of old malt, I look at their wives. I eat them up. Worse: I ogle. I am not normally given to ogling, but tonight, ogling is on the agenda. Blonde, brunette, plump, lean, their long legs rippling underneath satin and silk, their muscular arms trained by hours of top-notch tennis on private courts, they are sublime. Balzac, who shared my passion for the Touraine, wrote longingly, in *La Femme de trente ans*, of women over thirty. Honoré, *mon ami*, I'd settle for women over forty any day. *Il n'y a pas doute.* I am under the spell of the lascivious *Lochoises* . . .

The light is suddenly switched back on and my fantasising rudely interrupted. It's time to go. Outside, the night air is balmy and we all congregate to say goodbye. I am in a tricky situation. I can hardly say *ciao* and jump into the Mazda. They'd think I was nicking the street furniture. Things are made even worse when Amorosa, the cornflour queen, having cleaned and washed up, comes out and drives away in hers.

I am suddenly inspired. Instead of leaving immediately, I announce to the assembled company that I am going to have a midnight stroll in the old town. This has a triple advantage. First, I don't have to own up to the geisha. Second, the ladies find me even more romantic. Third, it pisses off the dentists. As I walk away, I play my final trump card. I recite a few lines from the poet Alfred de Vigny, who was born in Loches:

Gémir, pleurer, prier, est également lâche.
Fais énergiquement ta longue et lourde tâche
Dans la voie où le Sort a voulu t'appeler.
Puis après, comme moi, souffre et meurs sans parler.

Precisely what the meaning of these lines is I'm none too sure. I learned them at school in 1892. They have strictly no bearing on the present circumstances – no one, after a delightful dinner, seems to be particularly keen on dying in stoic silence, apart from the *garçons* annihilated by the Malkovich effect. Not only can he garden, he can recite. I can hear their teeth gnashing in the dark.

Loches is even more beautiful by night. Surrounded by turrets and silence, centuries melt away. The beauty of it all is breathtaking. As is the beauty of my hostess. In a delicate, orchestrated movement towards the end of the evening we had reached for a book at the same time and our hands had met, her soft skin brushing against mine.

Ping!

Merde.

The hatchback is up to its old tricks again.

12

Action.

If Malkovich can grow sexy vegetables, why not me?

I pushed open the door of the Toison d'Or like Gary Cooper entering a saloon. No one looked up. This time I was not offended. The Argonauts never do. If President Chirac entered and ordered a *suze cassis*, they wouldn't look up. If Sophie Marceau came in in thigh-high boots to buy a *morpion*, ditto. Looking up would be to confess that life is boring. An impossible thought at the Toison d'Or. Everyday life with its swift succession of pastis, flies, and cards is more than enough. A *rosbif* has not a hope in hell of attracting their attention. I am a mere ectoplasm. Had I been a hectolitre I might have had more chance of making an impression. I went straight to the point.

'I'm looking for someone to give me a hand with the garden.'

I knew them all by name now. There was Penthouse, so named after a centrefold, ripped off the door of his garden shed by a freak wind, landed in the school playground; Le Père Tubard, who, with the precision of an African explorer, is in the process of tracing the path of a new varicose vein up his left leg for La Veuve Cognette, the café owner; Nestor the baker, with his yeast in a plastic bucket at his feet; and Pois Chiche, author of the Venezuelan flowerbed.

Enter Henri, his nose looking more like a purple truffle every day. When he worked as a roof carpenter, Henri drank milk. Now, the village holds, he only drinks milk when the cows have been eating grapes. The way he walks is a reminder of what he used to do for a living. Balance was once essential because of the drop. Now it is essential because of the booze. Terra firma has become one immense tightrope.

Repetition is necessary.

'I need someone to help me with the garden.'

Silence.

'*Ben, c'est que . . .*'

Still no i's.

'*Il cherche quelqu'un.*'

'*Et il n'est pas le seul.*'

It took me a moment to understand that 'he' was 'me'. Odd. They talk of me in the third person. Perhaps etiquette requires it. I decide to continue in the same vein.

'He's looking for someone to help him with his garden.'

I show them my blister.

'He's hurt himself.'

Indeed, his blister is causing him some pain. They seem to be compassionate. He leaps into the breech.

'He'd like to meet someone who'd give him the odd tip or two.'

Here they are dubious, not to say cynical.

'*Ça.*'

'*Ah, ça.*'

'*Ça!*'

'Ça' seems to be asking for a bit too much. To find someone in the vicinity, in this rural area, to give you a hand with a vegetable garden? You've got another think coming, Monsieur Sadler. The paradox is acute. They, of course, because it is in their blood, because their grandparents knew, and their great-grandparents knew even better, they know how to dig, sow, plant, harvest. But they don't practise their art any more. They could. But they won't. Life, for them, is now nothing but Ricard and *farniente*. Of course I could try the younger generation.

'*Le petit Denoël. Lui, peut-être.*'

No good. He's studying law in Tours. And that's the problem. The children of *paysans* have all abandoned the land. They're all in their seventeenth year of a medicine degree in Angers. Or they've discovered they can earn more on the dole. Looking like one of Jean-Luc Mabillon's organic cauliflowers, Henri gives me a devastating toothless smile, and says, in a literal translation, 'Why sweat your arse off digging a paddy field when you can spend the morning wanking in bed for the same emollient?' ('*Pourquoi se crever le cul à retourner une rizière quand on peut se branler au plumard pour le même émollient?*')

'Emollient' means cataplasm. Henri doubtless meant '*émolument*' – emolument, salary – unless young men in the country are paid in medicinal poultice. The Argonauts are in agreement. My only chance – but it is a long shot – is Le Père Jules. Le Père Jules is an ace gardener. He's kept a notebook of what he planted, when and how, since 1932. But Le Père Jules is a prima donna.

I had heard of him. He has an orchard on the outskirts of the village. At first I had thought it was a camping site. Whenever you drive past there's a terrible din coming from down among the trees, an army of transistors blaring out different kinds of music – Barbara, NTM, Alain Souchon. I had a mental picture of what it must be like – young wives in pink Damart housecoats doing the washing-up in a plastic bucket while their husbands, in their boxer shorts, shave in a mirror nailed to an apple tree.

Nothing of the sort. The transistor is Le Père Jules' scarecrow. He puts them everywhere. The crow moving in on a ripe cherry understandably hesitates when it gets the impression that there's a rapper with a baseball bat perched among the branches. Le Père Jules' orchard is full of transistor trees. I was keen to meet him.

I was in luck. That very afternoon I heard the distant chugging of his ageing grey Mobylette moped on the road running past the farm of Aimé Matou.

'*Oh, les salauds . . . les salauds . . .*'

What bastards? Jules was not in the best of moods. His orange crash helmet, worn at a jaunty angle, had slipped down over one eye. The other eye, which he doubtless uses for driving – although his trajectory up the drive didn't necessarily confirm the conjecture – was sparkling with malice.

'*Les salauds.*'

The object of his anger? The employees of the District Council, who come round once every six months with a lorry full of tar to fill in holes in the road surface damaged by the passage of tractors. They only make things far worse.

'*Des fumiers . . . des fumiers . . .*'

Le Père Jules lifts his Mobylette up on to its stand, undoes the leather strap around his saddlebag and takes out an unlabelled green bottle.

'*Au moins, celle-là, ils l'auront pas les salauds.*'

Oh my God. I only wish they had got their hands on it. I don't want any. I don't want to taste it. The last time I had *gnôle* I couldn't speak for three weeks. This is a *tord boyaux* – a bowel twister – of the first water. Although water hardly comes into it.

'*On va boire un petit coup . . .*'

'No, really I—'

There's gnôle getting out of it. Firewater is a prelude to gardening. He switches on a transistor in the bottom of the left-hand pannier – maybe he thought a buzzard might nick his Mobylette – goes into the kitchen, sits down at the table and opens the bottle with the screwdriver in his penknife. He hasn't taken his crash helmet off. If I'm going to drink this stuff maybe I'll need one too. He grins and winks with his one visible eye.

'*Les salauds . . .*'

And pours generously. In order to avoid drinking I blather on.

'I am so very pleased to see you, Père Jules,' which comes out something like '*De vous voir ici cet après-midi me procure un vrai bonheur*'. The more elaborate the syntax, the less time there is for boozing. And I press on, pointing out how extravagantly difficult it is to find someone to give you a hand with your garden in the country. They're all studying at the *faculté* in Tours, it seems . . .

I'm in luck. The eye begins to twinkle again.

The Faculté de Tours? Le Père Jules apparently built it single-handed. That was when he was working for *l'entreprise* Baugé—

'*Les salauds!*'

And for the next hour or two, he regaled me with a first-hand description of the cubic kilometres of reinforced concrete he had laid for the aforementioned builder. Fortunately – because I do not possess sufficient technical vocabulary to follow the niceties of the operation – Le Père Jules mimed the whole business, proving himself to be the Marcel Marceau of the concrete slab.

All this heavy work gives us a thirst. Every twenty cubic metres or so we stop for a swig. The bottle is half-empty when the third Readymix lorry arrives.

'*Les salauds!*'

In the early afternoon I have the honour of being present at the opening of the pedestrian bridge which spans the campus. Very sadly I haven't time for the riveting story of the rest of the construction work, because – as I point out to Le Père Jules as I lead him back to his Mobylette – the Queen of England has asked me to tea and, even for Le Père Jules and *l'entreprise* Baugé, I can hardly turn the Crown down. I lift him bodily back on to the machine, point him and the transistor in the right direction and Le Père Jules leaves, heading back down the path in heated conversation with the cherry trees which he only just manages to avoid.

'*Les salauds.*'

I then retire to bed having taken nine anti-*gnôle* tablets. In the middle of the night I wake up with a start. What's that noise? Le Père Jules jumping down like a suicidal *souris* from the main beam? I calm down and return to my senses. Fragments of memories of the afternoon come back to mind. I seem to remember that he promised me a very special goats' cheese. The only way to age them properly is to lay them out in the ashes of a dead fire and to douse them in widow's urine. *Les arroser d'un pipi de veuve?* I take a tenth tablet.

The next morning I ring Gossard the mayor and explain my predicament. He advises me to contact the *Centre médico-pédagogique* in Ligueil. The team arrives the same day, smiling, happy and enthusiastic. There are four of them: Tronço (a chainsaw is *une tronçonneuse*), who only likes trees horizontal; Gérard, with his thick tortoiseshell glasses and his baseball cap, the Michael Schumacher of the Rotovator; Napalm, the king of the crop sprayers; and Georges the mower, who can transform grazing land into an instant Wimbledon but who has to be turned around every so often otherwise he will harvest the neighbour's wheat field. They all call me Roger. The afternoon passes in a flash. And when they leave, the work is done. The place is *nickel* at last. Neat and tidy.

I breathe a French sigh of relief.

Ouf.

13

Since I arrived, the conversion work on the barn has gone ahead fitfully. The pneumatic dibber returns on odd days, makes a few holes in the wall and leaves the work unfinished. It's a domino situation. The carpenter can't work before the plumber, the plumber before the electrician, the electrician before the stonemason, the mason before the carpenter and you're back where you started – *la boucle est bouclée*. They come, they get down to work, they down tools and they leave to do exactly the same somewhere else.

It's a cast of four.

Eric is the P (*Président*) D (*Directeur*) G (*Général*) of M (Moineau) E (*Electricité*) G (*Générale*) of which he is also the sole employee. Eric is multi-functional: central heating, plumbing, chimney sweeping and septic tanks. He drives an off-white Renault van, the rear of which he has equipped with an intricate system of shelves and boxes. In theory, small things go into the boxes and long things on to the shelves. At present everything – taps, pipes, bits of boilers, tools, pumps, nuts and bolts – is on the floor. On the inside of the back left-hand door, there is a pin-up of a pneumatic blonde wearing satin underwear and a fireman's helmet advertising a new silicone lubricant.

Eric has at present some thirteen or so clients in hand: four bathrooms, a pump down a well, five septic tanks, two central heatings and a leak. In all, some seven kilometres of piping. Prior to being his own boss Eric used to hang about during the day before doing most of his work moonlighting in the evening. Now that he has his own business, he has to work like mad during the day to prevent his old boss from moonlighting back.

For the excavation specialist Serge Leroi TTT (*Terrassement Tout-Terrain*), getting bogged down is no metaphor. Serge is one of the world's great boggers, a real pro. He'll bog you down an eight-ton JCB at the drop of a hat. If proof of his talents were needed, well over half of his fleet is at present immobilised in the – admittedly soggy – Touraine countryside. And as, in order to extract a digger, the second digger has to reverse at high speed, the extracting process of (1) often involves the bogging-down of (2). The rest of his time Serge spends behind the wheel of his sleek four-wheel-drive, zooming about the countryside keeping his clients up to date on the debogging of his excavators.

Antoine Mestre is the boss of a PME (*Petites et Moyennes Entreprises*), employing four craftsmen, specialising in carpentry and woodwork. Normally five carpenters means ten hands which means ninety fingers and ten thumbs. Not so in the Mestre organisation. Fatigue, carelessness, bad luck, and libidinous peeks at secretaries in short tight skirts picking up a wayward pencil have taken their toll. If the workforce formed a band, there would be few guitarists.

Jean-Charles Tignes, the roofing specialist, is known as Charly *la Charpente*. He has three mobile phones and spends a good deal of his time phoning himself: '*Merde! C'est moi.*'

Charly's passion is cycling. At home he has an old chest literally stuffed with his cups. You open the aptly named cupboard in the kitchen looking for a pastis glass and trophies rain down on the floor. Charly is fearless.

If proof were needed of his bravery, he is often to be seen walking over the roof on crutches. He knows what pluck means.

He needs to. The life of these artisans has recently become hell. Since the government decided to lower the TVA (VAT) to 5 per cent, and since the adoption of the euro, which encouraged the *paysans* to spend all the francs they'd been keeping under their beds for years, they have too much work. Everyone wants them: schools, town halls, retirement homes, me. And they daren't say no. If you say no, the client is going to turn to another supplier. The fact that other suppliers don't exist doesn't stop them from accepting everyone and everything. Result? Blind panic.

Yesterday Eric and Antoine both turned up. Their phones never stopped ringing.

'Tomorrow? *Sûr. A neuf heures. Juré.*' I promise.

'The day after tomorrow? *Sûr. A neuf heures. Juré.*' I promise.

'Yesterday? *Sûr. A neuf heures. Juré.*' I promise.

They are always on the move, phone stuck to their ear, sweating and swearing and leaving, as they rush past, a vague smell of chip fat, a vestige of last night's meal eaten too fast too late on a table covered in unfinished estimates. High spot of the morning, they walked into each other. They had two hectares of empty space in which to avoid each other and they collided.

'*Bordel!*'

'*Tu peux pas faire attention!*'

Discipline is called for. So as not confuse their tools when they share a job they use distinctive markers. Charly's chainsaw has a green sticker, Serge the bogger's a yellow one. But Antoine has just taken on an apprentice who is colourblind. Stress and more stress.

I met their wives. In the early evening I parked outside their unfinished *pavillons* – like that of Monsieur Dumas, often perched on a hump, the garden invaded by a broken-down trailer they promised to fix, a pile of wood waiting to be stacked and some breeze blocks that were once meant to become hutches for long-dead and eaten rabbits. Under the steps leading to the front door, the garage. No room for the car. It's stacked high with old washing machines and superannuated tumble dryers. The door is opened by a thin, nervous, attractive blonde who smokes cigarette after cigarette, who understands the endless stream of frustration and complaint which arrives on her doorstep and who would like to spend her evenings doing something other than typing out endless estimates on a flickering PC while the baby dribbles on the keyboard. The other kids are out of control. The twelve-year-old girls dream of sex and stardom and the boys of football and money. These are the Penelopes of the self-employed, ever waiting in the blue flickering light of late-night television for Ulysses the plumber to return home for a reheated *cassoulet*.

I have an idea. At the bottom of the drive I'll build a car park. The craftsmen will be requested to park and to leave their mobiles in the van. They will arrive at the house on foot. At the top of the drive a large notice: THE CRAFTMAN'S SANCTUARY. Once free from the pressures of the outside world, they can chat, have a pastis, play *pétanque*, relax. Visitors, if they so wish, can view them from afar through binoculars. On a fine, clear day you might catch sight of a painter with the blues, a salvage collector who's down in the dumps, a plumber who's cracked under pressure, a carpenter who can't make both ends meet or an electrician in a state of shock. It will be strictly forbidden to feed or to touch them.

And while the flock of happy craftsmen unwind on my verdant courtyard, I shall slip back down to the bottom of the drive and lacerate the tyres of their lorries. That way they won't be able to leave without finishing the job they started four months ago.

Et merde!

14

Ariane Tricot was really most embarrassed. Her children were so busy working night and day for their exams that they didn't have any time to allocate to me. She consequently decided – it would have been rude to bother me for nothing – to take some English lessons herself. Delighted to comply with Ariane's new-found linguistic enthusiasm, I suggested she select a literary text of which she was especially fond and to prepare a résumé of the story in English. We arranged to meet at the Café des Sports in Reignac, a small village some ten miles west of Toison. Did she not want us to be seen together in Loches?

Ariane arrived late. She had been to Tours for a vertical rock-face climbing lesson. Her blonde hair was still tousled from the shower and shone in the early afternoon sun. The rope had left a small blister on her left hand and she allowed me to touch it. Caressing blisters may not be in *Les Liaisons dangereuses* but its erotic potential is not to be underestimated. I noticed that the man behind the bar was eyeing us with a degree of suspicion. Doesn't he like people caressing wounds in his establishment? Or perhaps he was a patient of Brice's and next time in the dentist's chair would blurt out the news.

'Our ife wid ugh man who touch er blister *aiieeee*.'

Ariane, equally aware of the danger, decides we must leave. This is, after all, merely an English lesson. Not a lovers' tryst. The hood of her BMW convertible is down – she tells me the car is the world's most expensive hair dryer. She is wearing a diaphanous silk T-shirt and tight white corsair trousers. I find it difficult to remain pedagogical.

The countryside west of Reignac is flat and monotonous. As far as the eye can see, endless fields, the thin line of the horizon only occasionally interrupted by the hump of a farm or a crooked line of telegraph poles. Ahead of us, a vast ugly grain silo. A diesel locomotive pulling container trucks filled with corn is leaving the complex. A bell signals that the level crossing is about to close. Ariane puts her foot down.

'*Fermez vos yeux.*'

We only just make it. Ariane smiles.

'Difficult to live dangerously in Touraine. You have to seize the opportunities that arise . . . *Maï-quel.*'

The *Maï-quel* registers 6 on the Richter scale. Now, I have read my Marivaux. I am aware that in French – and particularly in the language of love – ambiguity is the name of the game. What am I to understand from what Ariane is saying? Am I an opportunity to be seized? I must be careful not to find innuendo in everything otherwise I am going to pass out every time she says '*oui*'.

My pupil abruptly pulls over to the left and parks the BMW in a large car park full of coaches and more sensible cars than hers. In the distance the noise of school parties squabbling and the smell of chip fat and grilled meat. A grandfather and a grandmother drag a reluctant child towards the paybooth promising presents. They wish they hadn't come. *Je les comprends.*

The Reignac labyrinth is hardly the place I had in mind for a one-to-one class in applied English. Why has Ariane brought me here? She explains. Brice, her husband, was the originator of the project. It was all his clever idea. She's so proud of him. *Tellement fière.* It's true, you have to hand it to Brice. He's managed to make money out of what must be one of the least picturesque parts of France.

I find the fact that people are willing to drive hundreds of kilometres only to lose themselves in a maize maze amazing. I try to translate my pun for Ariane but get confused.

We make our way through the throng hanging around the primitive mud hut village at the entrance. A vast hoarding advertises this year's theme: 'Plunge into the heart of the Amazonian rain forest. Discover its rites and rituals'. The weather is perfect for our visit – muggy and humid. A squadron of extremely large mosquitoes – bred on the local mosquito farm – fly past overhead, doubtless a promise of pleasures in store once we get lost inside. Emerging, as we enter, a group who have clearly been in the maze since early June. Pale, haggard, skeletal, they drag their exhausted bodies in the direction of the restaurant – today's special an *andouillette à la brésilienne* (a chitterling sausage in a thong?) – clearly delighted to breathe once again chip-fat redolent air of civilisation.

Ariane takes me by the hand. We advance with temerity into the jungle.

'Did you choose a text, Ariane?' I ask, seeking to cling to a semblance of calm.

'But yes . . . *Maï-quel*. I chose *Phèdre*!'

'*Phèdre*? I thought perhaps you might have chosen an English text . . .'

Ariane is disappointed; she stops, looks at me, pouts. She had expected a little more finesse, a touch more *esprit*.

'But *Maï-quel* . . .'

And she asks me two questions.

'What is my name? And where are we?'

What a fool. It all comes flooding back from school. Mr Pope and the Lower Sixth. *Phèdre* by Racine: second act. Phèdre, Ariane's sister, thinks her husband Thésée is dead. She is free to give rein to her passion for Hippolyte, her son-in-law. She confronts him and loses control. She imagines that it was not Thésée who descended into the labyrinth aided by the thread spun by Ariane, but Phèdre herself, descending into the maze to kill the beast accompanied by her lover on this hot, humid, Brazilian, mosquitoed afternoon:

> *Et Phèdre au Labyrinthe avec vous descendue*
> *Se serait avec vous retrouvée, ou perdue.*

Ariane takes me by my moist hand. Look. A plan. At the heart of the maze a secret grove. No one ever finds it. The perfect place for irregular verbs. As we move forward, plan in hand, she gives false instructions to bewildered schoolchildren wandering tearful, their hands clutching sandwiches and clammy boiled eggs. She sends a couple of middle-aged tourists down a blind alley, a Dutch family up a cul-de-sac. We are ever more alone, the wan voices of the lost fade into the distance.

At last we arrive at the very centre of the maze, a tiny islet of calm, remote from the world, inaccessible, secret, peaceful. Suddenly a movement behind us. I turn. I hadn't noticed a small bench ensconced in the undergrowth. Sitting on it, smoking a fag, is a Brazilian jungle inhabitant, his face painted in garish colours. Ariane lets out a little cry of terror. The bushman stands and quickly puts out his cigarette. This is a no-smoking jungle.

'*Excusez-moi.*'

He is tall, well-built, muscular and virtually naked. He then crouches, his eyes glinting, as if he has something important to tell us.

'I am going to tell you the saga of the rubber plantations.'

Ariane is put out.

'What did you say?'

I step in, dying to get rid of him.

'I'm afraid rubber plantations is not exactly our idea of an exciting afternoon, so if—'

Ariane in turn interrupts me.

'*Mais non, Maï-quel* . . . This is interesting . . .'

Interesting? I couldn't give a fart about the saga of rubber, but there's no accounting for taste.

'And just who might you be, noble savage?'

Ariane appears to be more interested in the third world than I thought.

'I am an Amazonian, I inhabit the jungle and I am going to tell you the saga of—'

The trouble with savages is that they go on and on. Ariane slaps him playfully on the fingers with her maze map.

'Don't be silly. I meant who are you in real life. What's an attractive, well-built young man like you doing in my husband's labyrinth?'

Handsome? With those ridiculous yellow and green stripes down his face and feathers stuck up his arse? All right, yes, he does have those rather vulgar chocolate-bar muscles around the solar plexus and his loincloth, unless he has cheated by using rolled Kleenex or Tesco's sausages, does seem to be reasonably well filled.

'*Je m'appelle Pablo.*'

'Pablo!'

The name is common but Ariane seems enchanted.

'And do tell. Where are you from, Pablo?'

'From Bolivia.'

'Bolivia! What a coincidence,' says Ariane. 'I've been sky-diving in Bolivia.'

'I adore sky-diving!'

And off they go on an adventure sports trip, pushing back their thresholds of danger. Pablo, it turns out, is doing a doctorate in anthropology at the University of Nanterre outside Paris. He whistles a secret jungle whistle and out of the undergrowth jump a whole host of natives, the one as naked, daubed and rippling as the next, waving their penile sheaths in enthusiasm. Who do we have? We

have Manuel, in his fifth year of medicine; Antonio, doing
a doctorate in linguistics; and Roberto, who is in his twenty-
fifth year of gynaecology at Acapulco, or maybe I wasn't
fully paying attention. They are bright, funny and
charming.

Les salauds.

A squadron of fat mosquitoes on a surveillance patrol
fly overhead. With an imaginary remote control I attempt
to coax them down to perform a Stuka-style loincloth
attack, but in vain. The applied English grammar is thrown
to the winds. I feel discarded and angry. The afternoon
ends in a celebration of Franco-Bolivian camaraderie. I
should invite them all for a drink around the Venezuelan
flag.

Journée foutue.

15

Bip-bip.

The yellow Renault post van comes up the drive. With a hypocritical smile on my face I leave the house. I try in vain to mask my bitter disappointment. Laetitia, the freckled, dimpled, irresistible Laetitia, was nothing but a dream of the past. Once again that fat grinning turd of a Bernard, as he hands me my magazine with old stamps on the cover, will keep me informed of the state of his health. Today, however, was different.

'Good news.'

'Oh yes?' I said, uninterested in anything he had to say. He produced a sealed envelope which he tangled tantalisingly before my eyes. I do not believe a British postman would dangle.

'*Une bonne nouvelle!*'

How the hell did he know? Had he been to work on it in his greasy kitchen with a boiling kettle and a paper knife, opening my correspondence?

'It's the communion of Cathy Coindre on Sunday. You're invited to lunch.'

'But . . . how did . . . ?'

Bernard looked at me with deep scorn. *Ces rosbifs . . . Quand même!* Everyone in France knows that postmen know everything before you open the envelope.

'Roland told me, Monsieur Stadler.'

He does it on purpose. He never gets it right. His lexical agility has been fuelled by years of groping around for letters in the bottom of Scrabble bags. Stadler, Satler, Sopler, Stopler. Bernard scores every time.

Back in the kitchen I opened my envelope, flattered by the invitation but angry with Bernard for telling me before I could have the thrill of finding out for myself. Normally you only invite family and close friends to a communion lunch. I had made the acquaintance of the Coindre family when Monsieur Coindre, or Roland as I now call him, had come to see me about his daughter's English *correspondante*. The young girl had not eaten for ten days and seemed to be in a terminal depression. She would shut herself away in her bedroom and play disconsolately with her mobile phone which, Toison being Toison, remained tantalisingly mute.

The Coindre were flummoxed. They had tried everything: *blanquette*, ragout, *daube*, pork, beef, lamb, horse, small birds, udders, noses . . . and she would neither salivate nor budge. What was up? Was she vegetarian? Muslim? Allergic? Anorexic? Macrobiotic? (There had just been a programme on the telly). Mad?

'No, Roland,' I assured him. 'The explanation is more simple. She's English.'

She was called Diana, after the princess, was thirteen and a half, tubby, spotty and pale. Her wardrobe would guarantee passing incognito in a massage parlour in Bangkok. She looked like a *boudin blanc* dressed for the Rio carnival. As sexual tourism has not yet hit the farmyards of the *sud Lochois*, there were only the ducks to manifest their enthusiasm, which they did by following the tarty *rosbifette* around, wiggling their feathery bums like a gaggle of courtiers on heat.

When I spoke to her in English she blushed with pleasure – the pale *boudin* taking on the more reassuring hues of the chipolata – and burst into tears. She was homesick. I had the remedy. I went straight back to the house and took from my own private store some medicine to cure her peculiar ill: a tin of baked beans, a pot of Marmite and some milk chocolate, which the French say should not be called chocolate at all as it is made from seal's snot, whale's bogies and artificial additives E121 and E122. Diana gobbled the lot. The farmyard applauded. In France ducks know what it means to have your face stuffed.

The young lady was reassured that, if she was ever in need of a fix, there was a dealer in the vicinity. She returned home happy. The honour of the Coindre was saved.

The communion lunch was set to begin at 12.15, when everyone would be back from Mass. I could see the guests arriving from Ligueil, the long trail of cars quivering above the blue-stemmed wheat in the hot air. When I arrived everyone had parked in an extremely orderly fashion, the cars at a forty-five-degree angle to the barn. This is the way it's done in the country. If a nuclear war is declared halfway through the *tête de veau*, at least the Citroën BX is ready for a quick getaway.

They were all dressed up to the nines: the men in their all-purpose black suits, the right size when they marry, far too small in middle age, and the right size for their funeral. The ladies wore dresses made of a shiny blue-black flowery material that clings to the underwear worn to obfuscate any daring transparency that exposure to the midday sun might occasion. In all, about sixty guests. I shook thirty hands, my fingers worked like a reluctant udder, and I kissed sixty cheeks four times, tickled by the downy moustache the ladies sport. Toison ('fleece') merits its name.

Everyone was in the courtyard apart from the two mothers-in-law, who couldn't stand each other. One was very proper, the other very much not so. The two matrons sat in silence under the awning of the Arab tent bought for the occasion at the local Jardiland (you could get one free if you bought eight 100-kilo sacks of manure pellets). With the wind in their moustaches, they looked like two walruses waiting for a gin.

Madame Coindre's mother, who had driven down from
Dunkirk the day before in her Fiat Uno, pulled me towards
her as I bent for the greeting kiss. She gave me a wink
and a chummy tweek of the left earlobe.

'During the war [wink, tweek], with all those RAF
pilots dropping out of the sky [wink], I gave a helping
hand . . . [tweek] But I wouldn't say resistance came into
it [wink] . . .'

Oh my God. Does she want to take me behind the barn
to bury my parachute?

The apéritif was served in the courtyard in the blinding
sun. A choice between Pernod, Suze, and whisky – one
of those special French brands like Clan McScotchy. I
entered into an interesting discussion with the only cattle
farmer present, André (Dédé) Lecoët. Dédé took me to
the fence on the far side of the courtyard to stare across
the pastures and to admire from afar, silhouetted against
the horizon, the impressive testicles of his bull. He gestured
as if weighing them in each hand looking like a pétanque
player choosing his *boule*. In admiring silence we mused
upon the vast amount of pleasure that Frivole – an odd
name for a stud – could give to endless unsuspecting
cows.

The apéritif slipped down without one noticing. I did,
at one moment, decide enough was enough and went to
put my glass down on the table when – surprise surprise
– I saw that I couldn't. The glass had a stem but no base.

'*A vot' santé, Monsieur Sadler.*'

And it's filled up again. You have to keep drinking in
an attempt to put it down.

'*Et encore un petit coup.*'

I popped into the house in search of a secret glass of
water. Roland, who is very good with his hands, restored
the farm himself. He has a passion for what is called *le
parquet caravane* – slats of wood interlocked and stained
brown to hide the beautiful old white stone underneath.

The whole place looks like a family sauna in an Ikea catalogue.

Sunned without from above and sunned within by the apéritif, we sat down at table under the Jardiland tent as red as cherries. I was sitting next to Madame Mortin, whose vast body is contained within the confines of a flowery corset, and Madame Matou, who is as thin and wiry as the electric fence Aimé erects around his cow paddock. They looked like Laurel and Hardy in drag.

We're clearly set for an olympic afternoon. The duck-shaped pâté has its bum firmly implanted in a thick wedge of Romanian *foie gras*. This is to be followed by *champignons* Greek-style, Cuban lobster in its coral sauce, spit-roasted lamb with *haricots blancs* and *verts*, cheese, *la pièce montée* (the assembled piece?) and *alcools* which I can't pronounce but which I can drink. Less a menu, more a marathon.

The English guest is eyed with circumspection and I am tested and taunted by the banderillas of long-festering myths and grievances: pea soup fog, the Loch Ness monster . . .

'*Et le Nessie, hein, le Nessie?*'

. . . and, of course, Joan of Arc, apparently the only Continental dish the English have ever succeeded in cooking properly.

They are right to be on their guard: mad-cow disease and foot and mouth have left their mark. With *le British* you have to be careful. They've been brought up on boiled meat and jam. Are they the kind of people you can sit down at table and have lunch with? I am out on trial. I represent the nation. At least the responsibility is sobering.

'Another slice of pâté, Monsieur Sadler?'

The slightest hesitation would be a diplomatic rebuff. I am honour-bound to comply.

'With pleasure.'

'*Et une autre. Avec un cornichon.*'

'A gherkin. How delightful.'

The ducks look at me with compassion. They know the feeling. And so it goes on. Another dollop of mushrooms in their gooey red sauce, another chunk of baguette, another glass of Sauvignon to wash it down.

'Come on, Monsieur Sadler. *Allez!* You're not going to leave that surely? *Vous n'allez pas nous laisser ça?*'

No chance of scooping up a few mushrooms with the bread and slipping it into my pocket. Every gesture is closely observed. As lunch progresses, moments of respite are afforded by the guests who stand and, in turn, offer a little entertainment. The stories are doubtless immensely rude – clear from the gestures and the cries of horrified delight – but unclear from the vocabulary, which at first I don't understand. I note down most of the mysterious words on a piece of paper – pausing only occasionally to seek enlightenment from my neighbours.

'*Zigounette* takes two t's, Madame Grellet?'

Later I recovered the crumpled vocabulary list from the pocket of my well-worn linen suit. I now know a tidy number of words for the male sexual organ: *quéquette*, *queue*, *zob*, *zizi*, *zigounette*, *pipeau*, *flûte*, *bite*, etc. Extremely handy.

It was my turn. All the guests seemed to have a host of stories to tell. Sadly not me. I can never remember jokes. Or rather I can only remember bits of jokes – the occasional set-up, usually about nuns, Irishmen, Englishmen and Scotsmen going into a pub – and the occasional punchline, such as 'Never after a milkshake Mrs Anderson!' But the two never meet; the head never fits the body.

Suddenly it comes back to me. Recently I read in the *Guardian* what was supposed to be the funniest joke in the world. Holmes and Watson are on a camping holiday. One night they go to bed and look up at the stars. Holmes observes the universe and asks Watson what he deduces from the spectacle. Watson mutters something about the

grandeur of the firmament and of the infinitesimal small-
ness of man and asks in turn:

'And you, Holmes? What do you deduce?'

'Elementary, my dear Watson,' replies the master. 'I
deduce that someone has stolen our tent.'

I tell the story in hesitant translatese but when I get to
the punchline—

'*On nous a volé la tente.*'

—no one seems to have understood. Roland comes to
my rescue.

'*Ah, ces Anglais. Toujours des histoires de tantes . . .*'

Everyone falls about. I'm delighted but mystifed. *Tente?*
Tante? I wasn't talking of aunties. Later I am told. '*Tante*'
means 'poofter'. Holmes would have been intrigued. The
meal resumes. Camille Baillou tells me about his first tractor
bought in 1959, Elie Tinant about fishing a stag from the
lake, Théophile Poupeau explains how to make faggots.
The *gigot* is raw and it's pretty tricky carving uncooked
meat while holding a glass of wine in your left hand.
Madame Mortin has discovered the secret. In order to
extract a sliver of lobster cartilage which is still jammed
between her two front teeth, she upturns the glass while
it's still full.

A cry of horror.

'*Les péteux!*'

The farters? Don't they mean 'starters'?

'*On a oublié les péteux.*'

We've forgotten the farters? Plates bearing kilos of
steaming beans appear from the depths of the kitchen.
Dédé gives me a nudge.

'We won't need petrol to get home this evening!'

Towards the end of the meat course, around teatime,
angry voices are heard. Roland is, in normal circumstances, a very quiet, reserved person, but, from time to
time, if the harvester falls on a stone, or the muck-spreader
jams, or the tractor sinks into the mud, I catch sight of

him in a distant field swearing, gesticulating, giving vent
to a deep, atavistic anger. This afternoon, a lamb bone in
his right hand, he is laying into his brother-in-law, who is
a rep for a firm of Japanese photocopiers. They disappear
into the kitchen and come out some ten minutes later, arm
in arm. The inheritance has clearly been settled. The
grandmothers, filaments of *rillettes* clinging to their moustaches like medieval banners, continue the struggle of the
clans.

'Of course Eugénie, at your age, I quite understand, it
must be very difficult . . .'

The children, with their greased hair, bow ties, party
frocks and ribbons have, until now, been extraordinarily
well-behaved. With the arrival of the dessert, all hell is let
loose. They chase the ducks, climb the trees and play football with a ball of dried cow's dung. The little boys pee
from the height of the tractors down on to their little
pigtailed cousins who seem stunned, gazing with wonder-
ment at the beauty of the fountain and at the mystery of
its source.

Music blares out from the CD player in Roland's huge
Massey Ferguson. I dance with Mathilde, the grandmother
from Lille, who sweeps me into her arms and explains
that although she drives a Fiat Uno she's always dreamed
of a much larger engine. Dédé Lecoët jumps on to the
table and begins a suggestive dance with a huge luminous
zizi – an inflatable sausage balloon equipped with a flashing
light – which he has pinned to the front of his trousers.
He wraps it round his waist, he uses it as a skipping rope,
he gives it to the girls to play with. The rhythm is wilder
and wilder.

Calm only returns with the arrival of the *pièce montée*
– which turns out to be a gigantic dessert made of a pyramid
of *choux à la crème* coated in thick caramel. The calm
has less to do with the majesty of the construction and
more to do with the complexities of its consumption. It

is all a question of the National Health and teeth. Farmers are very poorly reimbursed for dentistry by the *sécurité sociale*. The *pièce montée* therefore represents at once a temptation and a danger. The caramel might dislodge from their cavities fillings carefully put in place in the 1950s. The silence around the table is a sign of concentration. The caramel-covered ball of pastry will only release its cream-filled centre once the crunchy exterior has melted. No question of biting into it. Around me, in silence at the table, are sixty *paysans* who have all balanced the *choux à la crème* on their tongue and who are dousing it in saliva as if they were a human car wash.

'*C'est bon. Que c'est bon!*'

I stand up from the table with difficulty and look at my watch. Twenty past six! I'm done for. I've eaten everything. I've drunk the lot. My plate is clean, my glass empty. I've made a host of new friends. I've had a wonderful, unforgettable afternoon. It's now time to go to bed for a few days. Clutching the edge of the table like an alpinist to his rope, I grope my way along in the direction of Madame Coindre to say thank you and farewell. Claudette stands and I kiss her effusively about twelve times, both because the emotion is great and because it gives me an excuse to hang on to her so as not to fall over. A look of doubt dawns in her eyes. What's wrong? I thought I'd done it all, passed the test with flying colours?

'*Mais non*, Monsieur Sadler.'

Non? What do you mean, *non?*

She picks up the menu on the table and hands it to me. 'Turn it round.'

Turn the menu round? No problem. I can do that. Look. Easy. I've turned the menu round.

'*Lisez.*' Read it.

I can do that as well. Look. I can read menus. I read: '*Dîner.*'

I was just about to put the menu back on the table

when the reality of what I had just read dawned on me. Dinner?!

You must be joking! Not after all that! We've just had lunch. I'm pissed, stuffed, done for. What do you mean, 'Dinner'?

'*Lisez.*'

The menu reads: 'Celebration of the first communion of Cathy Coindre. Dinner: apéritif, onion soup, pheasant pâté and its nut oil salad, roast beef in madeira sauce, *gratin dauphinois*, cheese, dessert.' They're going to start again? An hour after having finished lunch? We're only half-way through! How can they do it? They must have been in training for years. All eyes are upon me. *Alors, le rosbif?* What about it? Eh? *Hein?* Going to throw in the napkin, are you?

I raise my head. There, clearly drawn in the white fluffy early evening cumulus, I see the head of the Queen. She is looking at me, a slight frown on her brow.

'Michael . . .'

'Your Majesty.'

'Surely you're not thinking of giving up?'

'Of course not, Your Majesty!'

I turn back to Madame Coindre, who is waiting for a reply. To sit down to a six-course dinner three-quarters of an hour after eating duck pâté, mushrooms *à la grecque*, raw lamb, a plateful of farters and twelve bottles of Chinon? Chicken feed.

'Of course I'm staying. In fact, I feel a little peckish.'

The company relax. *Ouf!*

Action must be taken. My body is literally full. Cheese is compacted in my toes, slices of lamb are piled up like carpets in my stomach and the little pâté ducklets have their faces squashed against the walls of my gut like football supporters against the railings. The first thing to do is loosen my belt, the leather of which is stretched to the limit and preventing the free circulation of goods. Another hole or two in it are essential, otherwise I am going to be cut in half.

I need a workbench. Do not ask why. Just bear in mind that my faculties have been somewhat impaired by lunch. The need is imperative. In order to make a hole in my belt I need a workbench. *Très bien*. Where am I going to find a workbench in a farmyard? Answer. In the barn. *C'est évident.*

Towards the back of the barn which stands next to the corrugated iron grain silo, I come across the much desired workbench, in wood, pleasantly aged and bearing the scars, rather like my stomach, of centuries of knocking and banging. I take a hammer and pause. There, to one side of the bench, lying abandoned among odd bits of agricultural machinery, is a soldering iron. Now, I have never soldered. But soldering, an activity halfway between plumbing and sculpting, has always seemed to me to be an attractively virile occupation. I shall use the soldering iron to burn a hole in my Marks & Spencer belt. Excellent. I doff the helmet used to protect one's eyes when soldering – I may be pissed, but I am sensible. I then undo my belt and release it from the loops securing it to my trousers. The waistband of the trousers, under the pressure of lunch, had slipped beneath the swell of my gut and the trousers fall down around my ankles. I am thus standing at the workbench in the half dark, hammer and soldering iron in hand, a Dalek soldering helmet on my head, my trousers round my ankles, when my hosts, evidently worried by the rather lengthy disappearance of their distinguished British guest, come into the barn and find me.

Silence.

An awful gleam of understanding invades their eyes.

'*C'est ça, les Anglais!*'

They are delighted. All their prejudices are confirmed. They have caught me at it. What exactly 'it' is, of course, they don't know; but they can imagine. The English are famous for 'it'. So that's what they do at the end of a long meal. They creep off into the barn, take their trousers off and, with a soldering mask on their head in place of the traditional fishnet stocking – in short supply in farmyards – they attack their genitals with a soldering iron. Jealous of Dédé's success, was I in the process of making myself a luminous *zizi*?

The new hole in the belt does provide some relief. I must now get to work on re-arranging the contents of my stomach. I lie down on the floor of the barn and, leaning on my left arm, allow gravity to cause the food still in transit to move downwards. I then do the same on the other side. If I eat lying down and roll over every three minutes there is hope that I can create some extra space.

Back in the courtyard my fellow guests are in full swing again, eating peanuts and drinking pastis as if they'd just arrived. I am very impressed. The gallic digestive system works on a twenty-four-hour basis. They must park their food like their cars. We sit down at table. There is, however, a subtle change of mood. As the dishes are passed from one to another eye contact is made. A challenge is issued. Look. I've taken some. Can you take as much as me? Pleasure gives way to resistance. We cut up small, we masticate, we eat slowly. Concentration is essential. At one point Dédé tries to get a conversation started.

'*Et le Toniblère? Hein?*'

But how can you discuss the Prime Minister with wit, intelligence and political acuity when you've got a ball of beef lodged in the left cheek and a puddle of *sauce madère* in abeyance under your tongue? Jackets are loosened, discarded; ties undone, discarded.

And gradually, one by one, the guests quit. They can't take it any more. They tie their napkin in a knot and, extracting their bodies from the table, retire beaten, broken, bloated.

There are just twelve of us left in the race. From the

depths of the kitchen where the losers are playing a desultory game of rummy, envious admiring glances dart towards the courtyard, in the direction of the valiant marathonians who are still at it. We look at each other out of the corner of our eye. There's no question of cheating. No slipping of a slice of beef in the back pocket, no concealing of *gratin dauphinois* in your shoes. You have to chew, swallow, digest, and on to the next mouthful. As on the final ascent towards the summit, every mouthful counts. The phone rings. It's the local doctor. He's on call. How are they doing?

'*Et l'Anglais?*'

L'Anglais? He's still in the race.

'*Quel courage!*'

And then the cheese arrives. And with the cheese, disaster. The Sainte-Maure goats' cheeses of Florence Mabillon, like the beautiful woman who makes them, are soft, creamy, supple, melting in the mouth. The Sainte-Maure with which we were presented after nine hours of non-stop eating, the last hurdle before the home stretch, was by no means mabillonian. It had aged for several months, long forgotten in the back of a refrigerated cabinet in the Super U. It was bitter, crumbly, with the texture and taste of plaster of Paris. It hadn't matured, it had dried up. You could use it to plug holes in dams, or to repair the damaged fuselage of transatlantic jumbos. In no way could you eat it.

The effect is devastating. The twelve contestants take a mouthful and suddenly stop, their jaws jammed together. Paralysis threatens. Alarmed, the spectators come out of the kitchen to survey with horror the totally immobile group of diners who have suddenly been turned into stone. Do we ring for the fire brigade? Claudette Coindre leaps into action. She runs to the cellar and comes back with a dusty green, unlabelled bottle which she uncorks and puts in front of us. No time for a glass. We are at death's door, our faces throttled purple, our eyes popping out of their sockets. I grab the bottle and take a swig. The relief is immediate. The cheese dissolves and with it teeth, gums and tonsils. What is this wondrous all-powerful dissolvant? Caustic acid? No. Far stronger: it is a bottle of *gnôle*. Roland's special *eau-de-vie* normally only used for starting tractors on frosty mornings.

The problem with the *gnôle* is that, while it clears the system with great efficacity, it also has a side effect: we are pissed out of minds in no time. Plastered, legless, *beurrés comme des petits Lu*. The end of the dinner is disgraceful. We fall in the tart, stick balls of *choux à la crème* up our noses, miss our mouths, dollop cream in the ear of our neighbour. Dédé climbs with difficulty on to the table and tries to repeat the lascivious dance replacing the *zizi* with an *eclair au chocolat* before passing out in the meringues.

A desire for gravity overcomes me. I bang on the table with my spoon, causing some displaced raspberries to splash rather violently east and west.

'Speech. *Un discours!*'

It is my intention to construct a literary conceit. Today two communions have taken place. On my right the communion of Cathy Coindre with the Catholic Church. On my left that of Sadler with France. But the words, queueing up in my imagination, seem unable to come out in the right order or in the right shape. They tumble out of my mouth like mad parachutists at a group jump. No one, including myself, understands a word. Who cares. It's the thought that counts. The ladies kiss me, the children kiss me, the dogs kiss me and my new friends, my brothers in *bouffe*, covered in tart and *crème chantilly*, hold me tight in their arms. The English love the French, the French love the English. The Hundred Years' War is over at last.

Vive la gnôle!

From the village down in the valley beyond the brow of the hill, one o'clock chimes from the church steeple.

Dédé's brother-in-law is a gendarme. Blind eyes can be turned. But I have no intention of driving the one kilometre home. There's no problem. My stomach starts just under my chin, finishes at my feet, I am totally ball-shaped and it's downhill all the way.

16

I rose early. The red rim of the sun peeking over the pastel blue line of the horizon had coloured the dew-covered blades of grass, making them look like tiny Arthurian swords ready for battle. In the fresh dawn air the village of Toison was a misty vision in the distant dimple of the valley. All that was missing was a rabbit with side whiskers nibbling a carrot in the vegetable patch and we could win outright the Walt Disney prize for tweeness.

Too much is too much. *Trop, c'est trop.*

France is too pretty. I have been seduced by its blousy charms. Everywhere you look there are castles, battlements, turrets, spires peeking through the fronds of century-old trees. Loches is a good example. Beauty left, right and centre. You can't get away from it. The architecture, the gentle curve of the streets, the old walls, the young mothers in shiny anoraks. *Assez!* It's too rich, a diet of truffles. I begin to long for an ugly village surrounded by bald fields full of jaded cows giving third-rate milk to make bad cheese.

I went to the Syndicat d'Initiative. The sprightly young lady in a blue suit and a tight chignon, doubtless a recent graduate of the Tourism School of Fécamp, greeted me with a smile.

'*Monsieur.*'

'*Mademoiselle.* Would you by any chance have somewhere ugly to recommend?'

Gulp.

'*Excusez-moi, monsieur?*'

She plays nervously with her Bic pen, on which is written 'Lovely Loches'. I explain that I am weary of picturesque France and that I am looking for *La France moche* – scruffy France, tatty France, the kind of place that no one ever wants to go to. Fécamp hadn't equipped her for loonies of my ilk. She smiled again and pressed the secret button to alert the *gendarmerie*.

And then, a few days later, fate did me a favour. Driving back from the southern-most reaches of Touraine, where I had visited a succession of breathtaking towns, one long string of medieval halls, romantic churches, rippling streams under white stone walls, I had a puncture at Donges. I quite liked the name. Donges sur Beuvron had a promisingly grotty ring to it. I repaired the tyre without too much difficulty – this was my lucky day – and walked into the village to look for a tap to wash my hands.

Donges is situated square on a *route nationale*, cut in half by a noisy, dirty artery. The pavements are high and narrow. The main street is concrete grey. When you walk down it, your shoulder rubs against the façades of the squat two-up two-down houses which have been weathered by years of diesel fuel. The flecked render has been especially conceived to create small cavities for deposits of dust and soot. The windows, framed in a lighter hue of concrete, and the grey metal shutters, caked in black talcum powder, are forever and mysteriously closed. The front doors, painted in a Ronseal oak-finish worm-proof orange, have a spyhole protected by two black wrought iron bars and a broken, fan-shaped glass veranda. The garage has slatted wood sliding doors with four round portholes so that the Lada will not wilt from lack of light.

The high spot? The EDF (Eléctricité de France) poles. Practically each house has its own – a rough concrete pylon decorated, to stop it falling apart, by ten metal rings circling it at regular intervals. The lucky ones get a bulky transformer thrown in. The poles have been chipped by the boots of repair men climbing up and down. At their base, the tell-tale discolouring caused by the lifting of the hind legs of generations of incontinent dogs.

When you look up, the blue of the sky is obliterated by a mish-mash of cable, as if a mad grandmother had decided to use the roofs and electricity poles to unwind a skein of rubber wool. The only splash of colour is the gable end of a house on which you can just make out the large faded 1950s ad for Du-Dubon-Dubonnet. In the dirty window of a *charcuterie* which has been closed for years, a fat cat dozes under a sign advertising *Boudin chaud* – Hot black pudding.

What goes on in Donges? Even in the remotest English village you'll sense latent activity. In Abesbury the inhabitants – men in cardigans and ladies with blue hair – are all members of the choral society, putting on a chamber version of the Ring Cycle at St Thomas's on Thursday at seven sharp. I bump into a few *Dongeois*, sporting the standard *bleu de travail* and orange crash helmet. You don't sense they are off to audition for the chorus in *Lakmé*.

The place has immense charm. This is just what I was looking for. Donges, an oasis of *moche* in a sea of beauty. A new *label* – a national award system – must be invented. The *label* for the scruffiest, the '*mochest*' village in France. This will be the new-style tourist trap. Criteria will be set out for mayors wishing to enter their village for the competition. It must boast at least one gigantic *château d'eau* situated as prominently as possible, a *zone artisanale* composed of five scattered corrugated iron huts belonging to local tradesmen, two of whom have gone bust, preferably situated in an industrial wasteland unprotected by a hedge, and, *le top du top*, an industrial pig farm consisting of flaky asbestos barns. If electricity and phone cables have been hidden underground, government grants will be made

available to dig them up and to put them up on poles
again.

The sound of a large lorry looms behind me. Monsieur
Poulet, the barbecued-chicken man from the Loches
market, is home from work. Mr Chicken only deals in
guaranteed 100 per cent industrial, non-organic poultry,
which he serves accompanied by calibrated, pre-frozen
reconstituted potatoes which have been gently simmered
in the suppurating yellow dioxine-impregnated chicken fat
oozing down from the grill. He parks on the asphalt wasteland next to the scruffy church with its chipped flagstones.
Odd to see him silent. On Wednesdays his *baratin* – his
patter – normally fills the market place: '*Allons ma petite,
venez tâter mes cuisses*' – come and feel my thighs.

Perhaps he goes out when he turns the flame down.

Two minutes later his wife comes back out of the house
and returns to the lorry. Slender, wearing jeans, sockless
feet in tennis shoes, her mass of auburn hair tied back
with a satin ribbon, she looks forlorn in the dirty high
street. She reappears from the lorry carrying two big
aluminium foil bags. They're going to eat one of his
chickens for dinner. For the last fifteen years, ever since
he set up on his own, they have eaten the leftovers, unsold
chicken after unsold chicken. You can see it in her eyes,
a sadness caused by diet of *poulet à la dongeoise*. From
a distance she looks like a woman desperately in need of
an intensive course in applied English. After battered wives,
battery wives, the listless spouses of industrial chicken
salesmen.

A lukewarm Pernod in a grubby glass in my hand, I sit
on the empty *terrasse* of the Hotel de l'Espérance with its
green plastic tables and chairs bought at the local Centre
Leclerc, its wooden Western-style saloon bar complete with
a blue neon fly-trap and an 'Alien 2' pinball machine.
Opposite, next to the church, with which it shares an electricity pole, is the shuttered house of the old mattress-maker,

whose faded sign is just about visible: E. Marceau –
Bourrelier. No one has stuffed a mattress in Donges for
many a year. I could move in, paint the place white, put
my AppleMac on the table and dream of Mrs Chicken.
From the first-floor window I would have a balcony seat
for the display of the *pompiers* on Armistice Day, on Mardi
Gras and for the 14th of July. But, best of all, I would have
my own electricity pole, the tallest, the filthiest, the one
with the most cables, which would connect me directly with
ma poulettière, the damsel of Donges.

The idea of such happiness wells through me. *Quel trou
sublime*. What a wonderful hole.

Je suis cuit. I'm done for.

Vive la France moche.

17

The *fête des jardins* draws closer every day. Tensions run high.

An example. For a long time I have been looking for a bench. To sit in the courtyard after lunch and to watch the clouds drift by is a very pleasant activity. The cumulus are the most inventive. Since my arrival, and with the assistance of the odd glass of Chinon, I have made out several pigs, a jug, a witch, the Queen, three Pinocchios and a rat with a moustache looking very much like Malcolm Hodge.

Shops sell only ornate rustic reproduction benches in reinforced plastic. Looking for the real thing, I decided to try the municipal tip.

The *déchetterie* of Toison is hidden away behind the corrugated iron grain store run by the local farmers' co-operative. I chose a cool day for the search, hot rubbish being somewhat repellent. When I arrived at the top of the tip, a lunar landscape unfolded beneath me: black rubber mountains of old tyres, a baroque garden of rusting metal looking like a Soviet bloc submarine cemetery, and deep valleys of household waste, as if the Alps had gone technicolor and started to stink.

In the depths of a canyon I espied one end of an old bench sticking out of a heap of compressed metal tins. I slalomed down the slope, taking care not to set off an avalanche of *maquereaux au vin blanc* and *sardines à l'huile*. This new adventure sport – muck skiing – required

precision and self-control. I must invite Ariane Tricot for
an afternoon at the tip. Once down in the bottom of the
gully, I found, to my delight and my surprise, that there
were in fact two benches – two wooden fins jutting up
into the sulphurous air. I pulled on the first one and fell
backwards on to the remains of several empty boxes of
Snuggies. Just a minute. I pulled on the second bench with
more circumspection. I was right. There were not two
benches, merely one bench sawn neatly in half. Odd. Why
would anyone wish to molest a cumulus gazer?

Using the two halves of the bench as ski sticks, I
worked my way back up the slope by means of the
western col – the *cassoulet* route – arriving at the summit
at 15.35. On the way back to base camp at the village,
I met Pois-Chiche contemplating the absence of falling
leaves and I showed him my bench. Pois Chiche was
quizzical.

'*C'est pas vot' banc.*'

Not mine? But I found it on the tip! Pois-Chiche nodded
in the direction of the village. The bench belonged to the
Chougras brothers. They inherited it from their aunt. Half
and half.

'*Cette moitié est à Arsène et l'autre à Gilbert.*'

Day by day, country *mores* become ever more clear.
Cutting a wooden bench in two and throwing the two
halves down the bottom of a cesspit doesn't mean that it
is not up for grabs.

Determined to have the bench at whatever cost, I first
approached Arsène. His small house in the village is very
dapper with its garden of red dahlias, proclaiming both
his horticultural and his political allegiances. In gingham
carpet slippers, with a Gauloise stuck to his bottom lip,
Arsène answered the door. I showed him my find.

'Arsène. I would very much like to buy this half of your
bench.'

Arsène looks at me, looks at the bench, shakes his head.

'*Impossible.*'

I indicate that Pois-Chiche indicated he might be willing to sell.

'*Cette moitié est à mon frère.*'

I went and fetched the other half which I had left at the gate. Arsène was perplexed. Why should a foreigner be so interested in buying half a bench? Maybe it was a Stradivarius?

'*Et mon frère?*'

I told him that I was approaching the matter in alphabetical order. Gilbert came next. Arsène explained his terms.

'*S'il vend, je ne vends pas.*'

Toc toc.

I knocked at Gilbert's door. The garden was full of blue flowers. Gilbert's carnations express public disapproval of his lefty brother. I showed him his half of the bench and explained that Arsène wouldn't sell if he agreed to.

'*Moi, c'est pareil,*' says Gilbert, pleased to refuse to enter a deal that involved his brother. He closed the door. *Clac.* So. One would if the other wouldn't, the other wouldn't if the other would. It was as clear as mud. Bench acquisition requires a clear mind.

Toc toc.

Arsène opened the door but less widely this time than before. I explained the situation as best I could. A gleam came into Arsène's eye. He, at least, seemed to understand. He could pull a fast one on his brother.

'*Je vends.*'

It was in this way that I became the proud owner of half a bench. A pile of old bricks now replace the missing leg. I could have asked Le Père Jules to build a new one in concrete but my body couldn't take the *gnôle*.

A few days later I bumped into Gossard the mayor, sucking one of his eternal indigestion tablets. I told him the story of the bench. Gossard shook his head and went pale. Apparently the Chougras brothers hadn't paid any attention to it until the village had the extremely dangerous idea of organising the garden competition. Last year Arsène won. Gilbert has simmered ever since. So when their aunt died, her will became a battlefield. Everything was scrupulously and mathematically divided into two. The china, the chairs, the tables. Gilbert got the bike, Arsène the saddle. Gilbert got the knives, Arsène the forks. Gilbert got the spoons, Arsène the sugar. When it was impossible to divide, they resorted to the chainsaw. A bed, a mattress, the bench were all sawn in half. The village was worried about what was going to happen to Nestor the dog, but Nestor, no fool, had the wit to do a bunk.

This was not the end of the story. Gossard beckoned me to follow him. Gilbert had taken a terrible revenge on his victorious brother.

We took the small lane which crosses the centre of the village and stopped in front of a pretty walled garden full of vast orange pumpkins. In the crepuscular evening light they glowed as if lit from within. I approached to admire these beautiful bulbous cucurbitaceae and was pulled up sharp, pixillated.

'*Nom d'une pipe.*'

One night several months ago, when these gigantic melons were merely the size of baby tennis balls, Gilbert Chougras crept into his brother's garden armed with a vegetable chisel. On the plump flank of each fruit he had carefully carved a letter. In the meantime the melons had grown tenfold and, with them, the letters. Almost invisible in March they now measure some sixty to seventy centimetres. One letter per melon, every eight melons a word. With the rather stunning result that the innocent passer-by is stopped in his tracks when he reads carved into the soft flesh of Arsène Chougras' melons ... T-R-O-U-D-'U-C.

A-R-S-E-H-O-L-E
Charming.
Gossard is thinking of twinning Toison with Corleone.

18

Today is the 14th of July. I bought a cardboard French flag in the Maison de la Presse in Ligueil and stuck it on the front door. Using, with some difficulty, the delay mechanism on my battered Konica, I proceeded to take a picture of myself, the house and the flag, a glass of red wine in my hand toasting the Republic. Aime Matou's cows eyed me sardonically. They found me a little over the top.

The 14th July Bastille Day celebrations on the Champs-Elysées are broadcast live on television. Unfortunately the bat who lives upside-down in the cellar must have absorbed a certain amount of the alcohol fumes given off by my Chinon. She (bats, like squids, are tricky to sex) must have been a little plastered because her radar system went wrong and she clobbered the aerial during one of her nocturnal flights. As a result the reception is snowy.

Keen to see the festivites, missing a bit of pomp, I am frustrated. Strange sepulchral forms move in and out of the pall of fog which envelopes the Arc de Triomphe. I take the bat by the horns. I stand in the middle of the courtyard and, like a baseball pitcher, take aim at the aerial with a tennis ball. The task is difficult: I miss several times but, the Robert the Bruce of the cathode tube, I traipse around to the other side of the house to fetch the ball and try, try, try again. In the end I score a ball's eye and the tennis ball lodges itself with some violence between the aerial and the mast, causing one to separate itself from the other. The resultant picture is clearer but at the same time elongated, as if the President of the Republic was standing in front of a distorting mirror on Brighton pier. Munching a packet of elderly Maltesers found in a drawer in the kitchen, I watch the march-past of a few brigades of elongated soldiers when the sound of a brass band playing 'Yellow Submarine' drifts over the fields from Toison. Tremendous. There is a ceremony going on. My longing for pomp is to be satisfied.

Above the war memorial in the village, the fly-past of jets has been replaced by a squadron of mosquitoes from the labyrinth. The process of '*désertification*' of the countryside has resulted in the phenomenon of *regroupement*: one priest for six parishes, one primary school for seven and one brass band for the *canton*. Brass bands, it is clear, only recruit from the physically unusual. The musical ensemble of Saint Senoch is composed of four apoplectic giants (percussion and brass), three pale gnomes (clarinet and saxophone) and a beanpole (piccolo).

The mayor, the morning breeze rippling through his crewcut as if through a field of grey wheat, places a wreath on the cenotaph, the three *pompiers* lower the colours, there is a minute's silence. After which the 'Yellow Submarine' leads us back to the playground of the primary school, where a warm *kir*, an *Oasis fruits exotiques* and some biscuits arranged in petal fashion on a cardboard plate await us. When you dunk the biscuit in the *kir* it crumbles and you have to fish it out with your finger.

On the football pitch on the outskirts of the village, the Club de l'Amitié have set up a marquee made out of scaffolding and the blue plastic sheeting used for protecting roofs during rebuilding work. Lunch is to be served in the sweltering tent – there is no shade – on a series of trestle tables and benches. A wooden dancefloor is in the process of being constructed next to two huge loudspeakers. A desultory dog crosses the field, pees against the electrical installation and moves on to survey the four lambs roasting on a spit over a trench dug especially for the occasion and over a period of three weeks by Pois-Chiche.

However tempting the Republican *méchoui* might be, I must resist. This evening Ariane has invited me to a party. I taught her the word binge:

'*Un "binge" Maï-quel, ça va être un sacré "binge"!*'

It was given by some friends who are the owners of the Château de la Planche on the outskirts of Loches. Bruno Petit has the local Toyota garage and Béatrice Petit runs a lingerie shop. Ariane assures me that they will be delighted to meet me. We have so much in common – the first thing, unfortunately, being a Japanese car (I make a mental note to park mine well out of the way). The second thing we have in common is the lingerie boutique. My eyes, tired of the crumbling beauty of old stones, often seek solace in the satin-filled windows of Madame Petit's emporium. There's nothing like a thong to revive an imagination depressed by the rigours of the dungeon.

Ariane gave me careful instructions. I am to take the Loches bypass and leave the third roundabout just after the shoe supermarket God'as. Then first right when I come to the pet food wholesaler Minou Soldes. The castle is just behind the refrigerated warehouse of the meat transport company Frigo-bidoche. The castle and its walled park, which until recently had been a sanatorium for depressed teachers belonging to the Education Nationale, is in danger of being engulfed by the industrial *zone*.

A present is essential. In Britain a bottle of plonk wrapped in brown paper would do the trick. Not so in France. You are up against stiff competition. A bunch of carnations can look meagre when faced with a Japanese floral explosion composed by the local *fleuriste*. Tonight I have a bright idea. In the shed I found an old wooden Bordeaux wine case. I filled it with earth and pricked out a row of mini lettuces, leeks, carrots, and basil. *Et voilà*. I'd invented the portable *potager*!

The Mazda carefully camouflaged in the rhododendrons, I extract myself from the car and take the box out of the boot. The other guests have already arrived – the apéritif is being served on the lawn in front of the château. Suddenly a terrible noise, like that of the furies descending upon an unsuspecting mortal. The back door of the castle opens and an angry horde of enormous Irish wolfhounds bursts out of the kitchen and heads towards my undercarriage with the speed and accuracy of a cruise missile.

What am I to do? Marooned in the drive hanging on to my *potager*, protection of the aforesaid equipment is by no means obvious. I tried to ward them off by clobbering them with the box but I am outnumbered. A bunch of rough pink tongues begin to devour me as if I were an ice cream cone. I've heard of the dogs' dinner but this is ridiculous.

'Boys!'

Fortunately both for me and the landing gear Béatrice Petit, wearing a little number she must have picked up at work, comes round the corner from the terrace. The shaggy poofters retreat, their task unfinished. They eye me with unquenched desire. *Le rosbif, c'est bon!*

Ariane peeks at the box.

'*Mais Maï-quel! C'est divin!*'

I hadn't seen Ariane since the Bolivian balls-up in the labyrinth. Do I sense a note of jealousy in her voice? The other lady guests, who are delighted to be enthusiastic, are bowled over by my miniature vegetables. They find me just as scrumptious as the dogs do. I'll tell Malkovich next time I see him.

Tonight is barbecue night. In the Stone Age barbecues were no-nonsense affairs. You came out of the cave, lit a fire, threw the chops on top and dinner was served. Not so nowadays. The Castorama catalogue offers a wide choice. First there's a huge fireproof breeze-block Aztec totem which looks more suitable for human sacrifices than for pork sausages. Then there's the Italian barbecue on wheels – *le barbecue de la flexibilité*, according to the blurb. You can grill your supper at the same time as you take it for a walk in the park. If the chops don't like the view, you go somewhere else. If it rains you can even wheel the contraption into the barn to the delight of the local fire brigade who would otherwise have had a boring evening at home watching television.

The Petit's barbecue is an American grill – a blue metal structure topped by a vast chrome dome boasting the stars and stripes. Brice is a barbecue expert. He has swopped his skirt for Levi's, a loud check woodcutter's shirt and red scarf tied cowboy fashion around his neck. Among the guests I recognise a gaggle of dentists and the Plantagenet who has a glint in his eye, aware of the fact that the last time we saw each other he choked on a peanut and dumped me in the early Middle Ages.

I am introduced to Bernard Bouille, who, apart from having an unpronounceable name, is also a sculptor. Bernard is squat and smiling, with a mass of curly black hair which, from a distance, makes him look like a fat mop. He is apparently a local celebrity. Two of his most recent works can be viewed in motorway lay-bys: *The Copse*, an evocation of the Loire valley forest, is a series of spiky structures in aluminium, three of which have recently been stolen, which led me to suggest renaming the piece *Copse and Robbers* but no one understood; and *Gastronomy* (lay-by number 23: nursery and *pique-nique* between Château Renault and Tours), a creation which, from the photograph, looks like a giant fork stuck into a bronze *andouillette*.

Bernard is in the process of consoling Gérard, the melancholic owner of a car-hire firm from Romorantin in the Sologne. Recently a client hired Gérard's wife and didn't bring her back. His is a dangerous business.

When I arrive Brice is preparing the fire. First question.

Are we going to burn wood from the forest or charcoal from the supermarket? The purists are ready to trip off into the undergrowth in order to collect twigs but Brice calms everyone down. In the boot of his Volvo he has the solution: organic charcoal. We all gather round and admire the bag. Bruno Petit brings out a pile of old copies of the local paper *La Nouvelle République* which we roll into tight balls. It's extraordinary how a newspaper becomes fascinating as soon as you start to roll it into tight balls.

'A *charcutier* from Le Louroux tried to strangle his wife with a string of *boudin*!'

'A vet from Preuilly took a hedgehog on holiday!'

Brice gets a little narked. We are more interested in the paper than in his chops. Finally the fire sparks into life but the direction of the wind immediately changes and Brice goes black in the face. As unperturbed as a surgeon, he calls for the chipolatas to be brought out.

'*Les chipos!*'

Amorosa appears from the kitchen with a large white serving plate and we gather round to admire her sausages. The wind turns again and now we've all got black faces. From a room somewhere inside the castle the ladies can be heard chanting:

'*Les saucisses! Les saucisses! Les saucisses!*'

They sound completely pissed and it's only half-past nine.

Life is cruel. Either the gaps in the grill are too wide or the chipos are too thin. Amorosa's chipos are of the geyser family. You put them on the grill, they fall through the hole, explode and emit a vast spurt of fat like an over-excited sperm whale. The resultant flames are so intense that we all have to retire and have a ninth glass of Chinon as we wait for the chipolatas to die down.

Gérard, who feels that existence is definitely ganging up on him, has discovered an amusing game. He places his chipolatas perpendicular to the grill and then tries to cut them in half to see if they are cooked. The result? Both halves of the sausage slip inexorably down into the embers. He does it again and again, taking a perverse delight in his ineptitude. Brice serves up the survivors. Burnt on one side, raw on the other.

'*Et voilà! Des chipos à l'uinilatéral.*'

'*Miam!*'

These are perfect party sausages. If you can't eat them you can always use the burnt end to draw yourself a moustache – Zorro, Hitler, Charlie Chaplin. I attempt a curly Dalí but end up looking like Carmen with ringlets.

'*Et les merguez?*'

Determined to be the perfect guest, I troop off to the kitchen. A bad idea. I had quite forgotten the hairy horde. As soon as I open the door the dogs make a second dash for my flies, ready to finish the job. Fortunately the fridge is only a step away. I grab a handful of *merguez* and throw them to the other side of the kitchen, hoping that spicy North African sausages will be an adequate red herring. The dogs are flummoxed, and skid to a halt. I grab the remaining *merguez*, stuff them in my pocket – munitions in case of a future attack – and make a dash for the door, leaving the famished hounds to devour the couscous accessories in lieu of my own. *Ouf.*

The ladies are still waiting for their chipos in the huge lounge with its flocked wallpaper and jingling chandelier. They have been waiting now for some two hours and are totally plastered.

> *Tous les garçons et les filles de mon âge,*
> *Se promènent dans la rue deux par deux*

Ariane sings the old Françoise Hardy hit, leaning against the jukebox, while the others play billiards, using their queues to remain upright. Several bottles of pink

champagne are empty on the table. They are delighted to
see me.

'*Enfin!*'

'*Un homme!*'

And they begin to bark in a novel imitation of the pack
of Irish wolfhounds. Automatically my hand clenches
around the *merguez*. The girls are in the midst of a meta-
physical conversation and they would much appreciate my
views. What exactly is the difference between *une pelle*
and *un patin*? I find the request somewhat odd. A '*pelle*'
is a shovel used for gardening and a '*patin*' a skate, used
for crossing slippery surfaces. The girls fall about. How
was I to know that the two words apply to different
versions of the French kiss?

'*Il est charmant, ton Anglais, Ariane!*'

'*Ton*'! I am thrilled at the possessive. Brice arrives from
the garden. The girls shreak with horror! He is caked in
soot and looks like an SAS man about to raid an embassy.

'Free us, Brice! *Délivre-nous!*'

And they wave their billiard cues in the air. Brice is
quite composed.

'*La viande, vous l'aimez comment?*'

The world is apparently divided into three meat-eating
categories. *Bleu* – meat which is virtually uncooked – is
very chic. Strange that to eat cold raw flesh has become
a sign of sophistication. The boys are *bleu*. *Saignant* – rare
– is not quite so top-notch but is acceptable. *A point* –
cooked – is naff. The ladies and myself are *à point*. Which
confirms the boys' prejudice. The *rosbifs* are an effemi-
nate bunch.

A terrible smell invades the lawns. The torch used to
illuminate the grill has fallen in the fire, plastic casing and
longlife batteries melting in the pig fat. But our hunger is
unimpaired. The grilled meat is accompanied by potatoes
roasted in aluminium foil. You place them in the embers
and forget about them. Not, however, for three hours,

which was the time it took for Blackface Brice to get his act together. The potatoes are like empty black coconut shells but are delicious with a nob of butter if you are partial to coal.

The highspot of any 14 July celebration is the firework display. The Petit have put on a splendid show. Everything is red, white and blue. For a fleeting second the whole sky is lit up with spurts, fountains, umbrellas, flowers and dervishes. We go 'oooooh' and 'aaaaah' and applaud every bang. A sky rocket lands very near the rhododendrons and for a moment I am terrified the Mazda camouflage is going to go up in smoke.

The pyrotechnic display has been arranged by the children of Bruno and Béatrice. As they are amateurs, there is a pretty long wait between each set piece and the colourful explosions make the intermittent dark seem even more intense. After a particularly striking firework, a huge geyser of multi-coloured sparks looking to all intents and purposes like one of Brice's ejaculating chipolatas, I sense Ariane's presence at my side, her perfume momentarily dulling the smell of smoke and gunpowder. I turn to smile in her direction when a hand, her hand, takes me gently but with authority by the nape of my neck and pulls my head down towards her. And there, in the pitch black of the garden, she gives me what I presume to be either a *pelle* or a *patin*. Her tongue explores my buccal cavity with the expertise of an accomplished dentist. Meanwhile her other hand runs down the length of my back and, in order to draw my body closer to hers, slips into the pocket of my jacket. Suddenly her body stiffens.

'*Beurk!*'

'*Excusez moi, Ariane, je*—'

'*C'est quoi?*'

She sounds disgusted.

Merde. I'd quite forgotten the *merguez. Quel con.* The spell is broken. Moments of magic are fragile. There's nothing like a cold sausage to douse the flames of passion. Worse, Ariane is going to think I was nicking the supper.

Whooosshh!

The sky is once again lit up by myriad colours which disappear as quickly as they dazzle.

'Ariane?'

I turn back to where I believe her to be, hoping to explain, but I grope the darkness in vain. She's gone. I am at once saddened and perturbed. What was she up to? Was this a challenge? A piece of market research? How many of the other ladies are at this very moment prowling around in the dark distributing shovels and skates? Suddenly a series of earth-shattering explosions announces the final tableau.

A moment of drama. A wild rocket lands on the car park of the nearby Centre Leclerc where bales of hay have been stored to provide crash barriers for Sunday's motocross. The fire brigade are quick to arrive and extinguish the blaze to the applause of the assembled guests. After their display they come up to the castle for a burnt chipo and a glass of wine. The atmosphere is festive but I can't for the life of me find Ariane. Gérard, the wife-hire man, eyes me with suspicion. Could it be that he had caught sight of Ariane and myself locked in a passionate embrace? Brice joins him. They seem to be conspiring. Maybe the Bolivian rubber specialists from the labyrinth had tipped him the wink or, as the French say, put a flea in his ear?

In backing the Mazda out of the rhododendrons in a quiet moment, I catch sight of Amorosa alone in the front room eating a plate of sausages she had fried in the kitchen, drinking a bottle of champagne and watching *Star Academy* on television. At least the staff know how to have a good time. *Vive la révolution!*

The football pitch in Toison is now lit by two powerful halogen lamps. The *Bal* of the Club de l'Amitié is in full swing. The dancefloor is packed with couples turning in rhythm in the middle of a huge field to the sound of 'Sous les ponts de Paris'. I am tempted to leave the car and to join them for a waltz and onion soup. But the firework display has disturbed my peace of mind, and I sit pensive behind the wheel of the car, watching the old lovers dance like moths around the bright lights of the ball.

19

During the night there was a violent storm, and the weather this morning is misty, clammy and moist – just what's required for my seedbeds. Soft, rich earth saturated with invigorating warm rain will bring the seedlings to life after a few weeks of general hanging about. I run down to the bottom of the garden with hope in my heart.

In vain. I am faced with a scene of devastation. The bed is bald, as if struck by lightning alopecia. One or two ragged lettuces survive to tell the terrible tale. The name of the apocalypse? Slugs. A horde of orange latex scavengers, attracted by the damp of the night, has descended upon my pubescent veg, passing heartlessly over them, eating them, uprooting them, flattening them like an army of rubber steamrollers. What is to be done?

Solution number one. I decide to be ecological and get rid of them by hand – or, to be more precise, because I don't fancy picking them up, by means of a fork. The technique is straightforward. You slip the prongs under the soft underbelly, lift them up and toss them over the wall into Aimé Matou's field. Out of sight, out of mind. *Ni vu ni connu.* However, after a while, this slug-tossing strikes me as futile. The soft scavengers will simply line up again and move in to rape and pillage as soon as my back is turned.

Solution number two. The Maginot Line. You take a bucketful of soot from the grate and you surround the seedbed with a black wad, a Berlin wall of dust, the ultimate

slug excluder. I'd seen Le Père Jules doing it in his garden.
I try it out. I put a slug at the foot of the wall and issue
a challenge:

'Go on, mate. Have a go. *Vas-y, coco.*'

The slug oozes forward, stops, frowns and gives up,
flummoxed. There's nothing like the sight of a flummoxed
slug to bring joy to the heart of the serious vegetable
gardener. Thrilled, I go about my business. What a fool.
I omitted to take into account the nocturnal passage of
the Matou mongrel brigade on their way to wreak havoc
in the compost heap. The inevitable happens. The dogs
trample the fortifications underpaw. The latex regiment
moves in. A classic manœuvre.

Drastic manœuvres are called for. After the mechanical
and the traditional, I resort to the industrial. Only napalm
will do the trick. Ashamed, I drive the thirty kilometres
to Chatillon-sur-Indre, where I won't be recognised, and
buy five kilos of slug death. The ad on the box is exciting
and repugnant. A salivating fat slug sits at a table with
napkin, knife and fork. The caption reads: *Son dernier
régal.* His last blow-out.

My colleague Honoré de Balzac, novelist and neighbour, who lived just up the road in Saché, wrote in the
foreword to his impressive *Comédie humaine* that, roughly
– *grosso modo* – everything is part of everything, the
smallest is part of the biggest, the microcosm of the macro-
cosm, etc. If you murder a slug, you consequently threaten
the balance of nature. But my loathing of their mindless
hooliganism outweighs any moral qualm.

On my return to the scene of the crime I open the lethal
carton by cutting across the dotted line and pulling as
indicated. I am about to sow instant death, apeing the
awesome gesture of the Grim Reaper, when I hear a car
coming up the drive – could it be the rapid intervention
squad of the local SPCS – the Society for the Prevention
of Cruelty to Slugs?

My visitors number three: she, pretty in a flowery summer dress; he, serious, carrying a black briefcase and holding by the hand his little daughter, complete with plaits and snotty nose. We pass the time of day. *Bonjour. Il fait beau.* What are they selling?

I am in a tricky situation. In my clenched right hand I have sufficient lethal slug pellets to apply for a job on Death Row. In order to shake hands, I have to transfer the pellets surreptitiously from the right to the left, taking care to wipe my stained *anis*-smelling paws on my jeans. I don't want to serve my guests their last blow-out. The little girl I kiss on the cheeks, thus avoiding any danger of having her slugged as well. Finally her father decides to play his first card.

'*La fin du monde est proche.* The end of the world is nigh!'

Merde! They are Jehovah's witnesses.

Where's my box? Not, I hasten to say, to repel them – rather to hide it. There it is: in the middle of a ravaged seedbed, its garish colours yelling for attention. I manage to conceal the lettering under my Wellington boot. In so doing I lose my grip and drop seven or eight pellets on the ground. Almost immediately, a juicy fat tart of a slug, turned on by the smell, nostrils akimbo, begins to dribble her way forward in the direction of instant death.

'Heed the words of the prophets: prepare thyself!'

Can slugs hear?

'Let those who have ears lend their ears.'

Precisely what I was trying to say.

'Would our behaviour be pleasing in the sight of God?'

Doubtless not, prophet, particularly as the slug is making amazingly quick progress. Only a few centimetres to go. It opens its big flaccid gob, ready to make a pig of itself.

'The day of Judgment is nigh.'

Precisely my problem. I close my eyes. Too late. Then, suddenly, I hear:

'*Papa!*'

I open my eyes. A miracle has happened. The snotty little girl has picked up the slug and is showing it to her dad.

'Put that man's slug back where you found it!'

I am quick to intervene.

'No no,' I say magnanimously. '*S'il vous plaît*. Keep the slug. *Gardez la limace. J'en ai d'autres.* I've got plenty more.' Millions of the buggers.

'*Dis merci, Charlotte.*'

'*Merci, monsieur.*'

Think nothing of it, Charlotte. Any time.

The visit ends with a prayer for the suffering of the oppressed community of gastropods and with the traditional distribution of magazines for lighting the barbecue. When the little Peugeot disappears back down the drive, I breathe a sigh of relief. I've learned my lesson.

I'll just have to sow again.

A nos graines, citoyens!

20

Buying wine in Britain is a pretty banal affair. You go to Tesco's, you do a little market research, you plump for a Bulgarian chardonnay at a knockdown price, and the deed is done.

Not so in France. The presence of the grower and the proximity of the *terroir* renders the oenological buying process a shade more complex. On my arrival, formed as I had been by the Tesco school of tasting, I simply bought boxes of the stuff from Super U, happy to score points which would bring me ever closer to a much-desired gift of six rustic oven gloves.

My world changed the day Brice Tricot served me a very particular Chinon. The wine was delicious, with its raspberry nose and its rhubarb-like asperity on the teeth. It had bite and class. In fact it was *canaille*. The dictionary says 'spivvy, roguish'. It was a rakish tipple – the kind of word you can use for wine which costs less than five euros a bottle. If it's more upmarket, the vocabulary follows suit and you move into the bracket of *bouquets*, *jambes* and *robes*. This spivvy Chinon was just my cup of tea. But it was the bottle as much as the wine – a bottle without a capsule and without a label, a bottle cool from the wine-grower's cellar – which seemed to me the *nec plus ultra* of sophistication.

I could, of course, have continued to buy wine at the local Super U and spent my long evenings scratching off the labels with a nailfile – but this would have been a cop-out. I took

courage in both hands and decided to address myself to
the fountainhead of this particular delight: the *vigneron*
in person. His name? Monsieur Gaston Bourru – or Le
Père Bourru – whose Chinon had supplied the Tricot
family for generations.

I phoned. An elderly lady told me to phone back. I
phoned back. The elderly lady told me he'd just gone out.
I phoned back. The elderly lady told me he'd be there
tomorrow. I phoned back. The elderly lady told me he
wasn't in and if it was wine I was after there wasn't any
left. I phoned back. He'd just gone to the doctor. Would
I ever find him? Persistence paid off and after a dozen or
more calls I made contact. I used what I hoped was the
magic password.

'*Je suis un ami des Tricot.*'

Le Père Bourru didn't even grunt, but he did give me a
rendezvous. I felt honoured. This cat and mouse game is
all part of the process. If you want it, you've got to work
for it. In my present frame of mind I would have been
ready to do Toison–Chinon on my knees to get my hands
on the merest lark's piss of the stuff.

Having used the Tricot in order to grease my way into
the good favours of Le Père Bourru it was important that
I didn't let them down. A little research was called for. In
the Maison de la Presse in Loches I bought a DIY wine
expert manual, a vocabulary book and got down to the
job: *chaptalisation* – the adding of sugar to boost the
alcohol content of the wine, named after Napoléon's
henchman Chaptal; *vendange verte* – the pruning of green
grapes in the summer to improve the concentration of the
remaining bunches; *fermentation malolactique* – the
Cinderella-like transformation of malic acid into lactic acid;
chapeau – the cap of solids forming at the surface of the
wine during fermentation; *pigeage* – the stamping-down
of the cap by hand or foot; *débourbage* – the separation
of the *bourbes* (waste matter) from the grape must; *cépage*

– grape variety; *assemblage* – the blending of wine from the same origins; *éraflage* – the separation of grape berries from their stalks; *pourriture noble* – noble rot, a brown mould on the grape caused by *botrytis cinera*; and finally, my favourite, *ouillage* – compensating for natural contraction or evaporation by filling up a cask or bottle with wine from another. The word in English is ullage but I've never been able to slip it casually into conversation.

'Hello Barbara, how's the ullage?'

D-Day arrived. What to wear? I settled for a badly ironed *bleu de travail* plus a shirt and tie – the chic *paysan* look. I arrived at the appointed hour at the entry to the *caves* in the courtyard of a *maison troglodyte*, dug out of and into the chalk rock face. All around lay the attractive jumble of the *vigneron*'s gear – barrels in the process of being cleaned, the wicker baskets used at harvest time, thick plastic tubes, empty crates, an age-old tractor with a trailor the inside of which was stained ruby red. This was what I had hoped for. This was a long, long way from the razzmatazz of Bordeaux. No museums, no public relations, no picture postcards. This was the real McCoy. Château Grot. All that mattered was the booze.

A movement behind me.

'*Bonjour, monsieur.*'

Maybe I should get down on one knee?

'*Vous êtes bien Le Père Bourru?*'

'*Ça se peut.*'

The great man himself, like Aimé Matou, cultivated ontological doubt as to his real identity. I was impressed by his presence and by his bulk. I'd never been this close to a *vigneron*. This one was square and squat. He also was wearing a *bleu de travail*, with a pair of secateurs in his top pocket, his fingers seemingly repaired by thick black sellotape. His face was as crumpled as a pair of sheets after a night of debauchery. I ran through my newfound vocabulary, wanting to make an impression, but found it tricky to fit malolactic fermentation casually into the conversation. I settled for a rather limp, '*Est-ce que vous avez du vin?*'

What did I think he might have? Doughnuts?

Le Père Bourru didn't deign to reply. He turned on his heels and walked into the *cave*. He didn't ask me to follow him but, desperate to get my hands on his nectar, I had to snatch at any straw. The smell exuded by the cavern was incredibly exciting. As my eyes accustomed themselves to the dark I could make out a most beautiful sight – a long line of barrels standing against the curved wall of the tunnel disappearing into the depths of the hill, looking like an army of portly soldiers. They were of all shapes and sizes – *des fûts, des tonneaux, des foudres, des barriques*. I'd learned the words but couldn't use them because he was already some fifty yards ahead of me. The high priest was standing by a huge barrel marked with illegible hieroglyphics in chalk. He knocked out the large cork – *la bonde* – with his elbow.

'*Ah, la bonde,*' I said.

He looked at me as if I was mad.

'*Oui, la bonde. Et alors?*'

I didn't have much to add as my purpose was to impress him that I knew the word and the attempt had failed.

'*Ah, la belle bonde.*'

Gentlemen prefer *bondes*, I could have added, but he didn't speak English. Anyway he wasn't in a mood for badinage. He plunged his pipette deep into the entrails of the barrel, extracted it with the flourish of d'Artagnan removing a rapier from its sheath, and splashed it into a silver *taste-vin* which he passed to me.

'*Goûtez.*'

Oh my God. There's an exam. I looked at him, he was looking at me – his lizard eye lurking deep and suspicious in the depths of his eyebrows. My tastebuds panicked. I had a sip. What did it taste of? It tasted like wine. I could hardly say, '*Il a un goût de vin.*'

'*Alors?*'

I had to say something.

'*Il est jeune.*'

'*Il est vieux!*'

Sod.

I muttered something about being very young for a wine obviously so mature but the pipette was already emerging from another barrel. Le Père Bourru was having a good time. *Il est con, ce rosbif.*

'*Et celui-ci?*'

I telephoned the tastebuds. They were hiding under the bed.

'Fruity . . . ?'

Wrong. Tannic. Next.

'Long and round?'

No. Thin and short.

'*Très différent du 97.*'

'*C'est du 97.*'

Desperate, my back to the wall, I played my last card.

'*Vous l'avez ouillé?*'

'*Ouillé?*'

He looked at me as if I'd gone out of my mind. I panicked and lost control. I told him that his *pigeage* was a great success. That my palate was impaired and that I'd doubtless feel better after a *débourbage*. Le Père Bourru didn't smile. He turned on his heels and walked towards the entrance of the *cave*. He obviously thought that *pourriture noble* had attacked my brain. I had failed. Nought out of ten. Why the hell should he sell his wine to someone who had spent his life drinking a stew made from dried leaves, who put jam on his meat and who accused him of ullaging?

Deep depression overcame me. All that work for nothing. I resigned myself to evenings of scratching labels. Suddenly a drama. A voice from the mouth of the cellar called out.

'*Vite! Gaston! Viens vite. Elle s'est sauvée la salope!*'

Had Madame Bourru done a bunk? Le Père Bourru, clearly alarmed, ran out of the *cave* and up the steep path leading to the vines above it. I followed hard on his heels, emerging from the darkness into the glaring light of day. And I came to an abrupt halt. There, in the middle of the courtyard of a dilapidated winegrower's troglodyte house a few kilometres east of Chinon, I found myself face to face with an ostrich.

In order to fail the Bourru entrance test I had only tasted two or three sips from a *taste-vin*. I could hardly be drunk. What the hell was an ostrich doing in Chinon?

'*Arrêtez-la, petit con!*'

From the vineyard above the cellar an angry Père Bourru was shouting down orders.

'*Hé. L'Angliche.*'

Presumably me.

'*Si tu veux du pinard, l'Angliche, va falloir que tu apprennes à attraper les bêtes.*'

The '*tu*' I presumed was derogatory. So this must be the second test. After the tasting, the safari. There was nothing for it. It was this or no booze. Throwing caution and animal rights to the winds I threw myself at the startled ostrich, stamped on its cap and destalked it. Then, with a deft movement, I did a malolactic from behind, and gave it a swift kick in the *bourbes*.

Le Père Bourru arrived, put a lead around its neck and led the ostrich gently back to the ranch, complimenting me as he left.

'*T'es moins con que t'en as l'air.*'

As I was less stupid than I looked, I was allowed to buy two cases, sold under strict instructions not to touch them for the next ten years. I waited a couple of weeks and opened one. Absolutely delicious. The perfect blend of raspberry and rhubarb.

Le Père Bourru I'd obviously underestimated. His

second-in-command explained to me. The farmyard may have looked messy, the equipment may have looked antiquated, but his boss had made a mint out of his booze. They used to serve it on Concorde.

The ostrich had escaped from his private zoo. He started with a few second-hand llamas. An anteater was arriving once it got its visa. If I wanted to visit he gave me the instructions: turn right at the barn with the eighteenth-century steam organ. Just before the collection of antique cars.

So much for Château Grot.

21

I am at a crossroads.

The Atac flier advertised a special offer: tuna fish in pure olive oil, three tins for the price of two; 33 per cent for free. A snip. I cleared the boot of the Mazda and drove to Ligueil early in the morning to avoid the inevitable mid-morning rush of tuna addicts. Stocks were high. I was in luck. As I began to fill my basket, however, a terrible thought struck me.

If I open, say, three tins a week for lunch – with a crisp green lettuce, garlic, tomatoes and an occasional slug or two of cool rosé – then I won't be needing a basketful. I can measure out my life in tins of fish. The calculation induces instant depression. Time is running out. When I pull back the ring of this tin, and I take it out of the basket to contemplate the awful thought, then I shall be on the point of leaving, my six months at an end. What is six months? Beforehand, a lifetime. Afterwards, nothing. A drop in the ocean. The time it takes for a blade of wheat to grow sixty centimetres. *Ren*.

In the country, each day resembles the next. You get up, make the coffee, squeeze an orange, toast the baguette. You read yesterday's paper again, pass the time of day with the leeks – Good morning, Michael, *ça va*? *Ça boume* – weed, hoe, avoid Bernard the postman, prepare lunch, listen to the news on France Inter, have a little siesta, attempt to crack *La Renaissance lochoise* with a dictionary, rescue the odd slug from instant death, do some shopping,

ponder – chop or steak? Cod or plaice? – open a bottle
of Chinon, dream. Time seems to stand still. But standing
in Atac with my basketful of tinned fish I have to face the
truth. The sands are running out.

Only five weeks to go. The words ring like doom in the
steeple of my mind.

Do I have to go back?

Yesterday I bumped into Monsieur Dumas and a group
of friends in the Bar des Sports in Ligueil. It's extraordinary. They all look alike. Zipper jacket, mole-coloured
suede shoes, beige trousers and tartan cap with pompom
lying on the table beside the Pernod or perched on the
zinc bar. Are they clones?

When I arrived they were in the process of telling each
other what seemed to be a hysterically funny story. They
all mucked in, adding details and falling about laughing.
I didn't understand a word. Monsieur Dumas winked
in my direction and led me off to the quieter PMU (Paris
Mutuel Urbain) corner – where you place bets on the
horses. He filled me in. They were plotting something
pretty fiendish. *Une sacrée connerie.* He could hardly
tell me about it. He kept stopping, wiping the tears of
laughter from his eyes. The others joined us to give him
a hand.

'*Cette année pour les Comices . . .*'

The chorus roared with laughter. The *comices agricoles*
is the local annual agricultural show in September. What
had they got up their sleeve?

'*On va construire un char . . . et on va être dessus habillés
en . . .*'

They were going to build a carnival float and they were
going to be up on the float dressed as . . .

'*Les Pom Pom Boys!*'

This was too much for half the clones, who limped,
cross-legged, off to the *toilettes* pissing themselves with
laughter. It's true. The thought of Monsieur Dumas and

the clones in short yellow skirts twirling their pompoms would be *une sacrée connerie*. But this was not all.

'*Pour le calendrier . . .*'

For the New Year calendar . . .

'*Les artisans locaux . . .*'

The local tradesmen . . .

'*Une photo de groupe . . .*'

'*Tout le monde . . .*'

'*A poil!*'

And they all hang on to each other to prevent themselves collapsing in a heap. I didn't like to suggest that their idea, however daring, was hardly new. It's quite difficult to find a society – from the WI to the Freemasons – not willing to take their clothes off for the Christmas calendar. True, the Dumas army in the buff, twenty-three plump naked gnomes, masking their manhood with a discreet tartan cap, would be a welcome addition to a dull kitchen wall.

The remaining clones crossed their legs and hopped off to join the others in the now jampacked public pisser. Sitting alone in the bar waiting for them to return, I meditated. They've got a point.

I need a *connerie* myself! Maybe it's the only way to stay? An idea. I'm going to write a book. The title? *Le Bar des Sports*. I'll travel on foot across France from top to bottom and in a straight line – travelling from Bar des Sports to Bar des Sports. Why? Because that's where it all happens. That's where France takes place. At the *zinc* of the Bar des Sports. That's where they talk about sex, politics, leeks, slugs. My route? Lille–Douai–Cambrai– St Quentin–Coucy–Soissons–Montmirail–Courgivaux–Provins –Bray–Pont sur Yonne–Sens–Joigny–Auxerre–Clamecy– Brinon–St Saulge–La Machine–Decize–Moulins–Varennes sur Allier–Vichy–Thiers–Ambert–La Chaise-Dieu–Bellevue- la-Montagne–Le Puy–Langogne–Villefort–Alès–Sommières– Montpellier.

In the evening, weary after a day's hike across the barren

causses, I'll hobble down into the valley to stop at the auberge for soup, lamb, a gratin, a bottle of red, to exchange a joke with the cook and to flirt with the sexy *pharmacienne* who sells me plasters and digestion pills. The next morning, after a coffee and some warm bread, I'll set off again back up into the hills, for another day's hike from *saucisson* to *rillettes*, from *boudin* to *andouille*, from café to café, movingly gently, slowly across *la France profonde* I love so much.

I ordered a bottle of Chinon to drink to the book's launch. Already number one in Lithuania.

Parquienne.

Bravo, *Maï-quel!* Cheers.

Merci, Maï-quel. Up yours.

22

D-Day is upon us. The village fête and the Best Garden
Competition are on Sunday. I rise early and go down to
the *potager* with my gardener's manicure outfit, ready for
a final grooming. Just a minute – something odd's happened
to my leeks. I get down on all fours for a more intimate
examination. *Ciel!* They're punctured by tiny holes from
which either dew or their life blood is oozing away. There
are a lot of things that can happen to a leek in its career.
It can go downy, white, hollow, it can shank and rot, it
can smut and rust, it can twist and shout. But a leek that
leaks?! This must be the mark of the dreaded worm. If
swift action is not taken I shall be obliged to enter my
vegetables for the lacework competition.

I take a couple of specimens from their sick bed and
carry them down to the village to await the return of Le
Père Jules, who is doubtless laying concrete in some far-
flung corner of the universe. Waiting in French slang is
poireauter. Extremely apt. He arrives in the early evening,
his wicked eye glinting out from under his orange crash
helmet knocked skew-whiff by one or two blows from a
bottle of *gnôle*. The professor examines the patient. His
diagnosis is immediate:

'*Les salauds!*'

There is only one remedy. I follow him into the front
room of the small house he occupies in the village, conveniently situated opposite the Toison d'Or. On the heavy
dark wood sideboard a stuffed ferret and two spare crash

helmets – one for Friday night shopping, one for church on Sunday. Without taking off the one he's wearing, Le Père Jules opens the cupboard door and plonks a bottle on the table.

'*L'eau de javel.*'

Disinfectant?!

He fills two glasses and passes me one.

'*Mais Père Jules . . .*'

Jeyes fluid for an apéritif is pushing it.

'*Les salauds!*'

And he empties his glass. Has he got leek worm too? I lift the glass to my nose. Oh my God. It's *gnôle*. I would have preferred disinfectant. I edge my way to the sink and, pretending to sneeze, manage to pour the *gnôle* down the plug hole. The contact with the cold produces a chemical reaction and the sink starts to steam. Fortunately Le Père Jules hasn't noticed anything. He has already retired to the kitchen to lay a concrete floor or two and I exit on tiptoe leaving him in animated conversation with himself.

Back at the house I experiment with his miracle cure. I immerse the two infected leeks in a glass of *eau de javel*, light the blue touchpaper and retire. The next morning the miracle has happened. No more leek worm. Unfortunately, no more leek either. The mixture must have been too strong. I am left with what looks like an albino pencil. By dint of perseverance and experiment I arrive at the correct mix. The effect is instantaneous and my prized, if not prize leeks recover their former splendour. *Ouf!*

Feelings are running high in the village. For the past few weeks excitement has been titillated – the process the French call *le teasing* – by small orange fluorescent posters nailed to roughly cut pieces of wood stuck into the soft verges on the roads leading to the village: a car boot sale (*vide grenier*), a show (*animation*), drink all day (*bar champêtre*) and – the high spot of the calendar of the Toison season – the *concours des jardins*.

Surreptitiously and by night I have been studying the competition. The variety is impressive: there are gardens full of vegetables on steroids, boasting beetroots and carrots straight out of porno movies; military gardens with the well-drilled regimental veg lined up at attention; hirsute gardens, bald gardens, epilated gardens, hippy gardens, ecological gardens full of healthy but minute members of the brassica family, and one mini-Versailles, with pebbled pathways, a dolphin fountain with a solar panel and gnomes in place of the equestrian statues. One gardener is head and shoulders above the others; the Hodges were not mistaken. Aimé Matou knows what he is at. How the hell can I beat anything as good as this? His garden is well planned, weedless, healthy and admirable. *Le salaud.*

In Britain, come Garden Festival time, it is quite normal for dibbers to be drawn. The polite lady horticulturists, with their Garden Centre aprons and woodlice-free, blue rinse hairdo, who have spent the whole year complimenting the neighbour on the beauty of his shrubs, turn overnight into herbaceous terrorists, using Round Up when the wind is blowing in the wrong direction, releasing cutworms and chafer grubs specially reared in small boxes in the garage and tossing paraquat over the garden wall while the Parsons are at church.

I toyed with the idea of bribery and corruption. The jury was composed of five experts: Gossard the mayor, who might be partial to a festive box of indigestion tablets; Madame Roubaud, who, according to a public pronouncement made on the waves of Radio Armpit on Tuesday 21st and rebroadcast in the evening of the 22nd, was very partial to dahlias; Dédé Lecoët, whose only predilection, according to my experience, were taurine testicles; Tubard, whose tastes were a mystery; and Le Père Jules, whose judgement could perhaps be knocked off course by a bottle or two of *gnôle*.

But then, two days before the competition began, in the

middle of the night, I had a better idea. No. Not an idea: a revelation. An illumination. A flash of diabolical brilliance. Torch and fork in hand I went down to the bottom of the garden where the leeks were fast asleep.

'*Mais . . .*'

I was delighted to hear that, even when rudely awoken, my leeks were bilingual.

'*Que diable!*'

Aimé Matou was tucked up in bed. I had to work fast while the coast was clear. It is essential that no one sees me. I took the fork and began to lift the leeks. The calm of the night was shattered by their cries of horror!

'*Michael! Qu'est-ce qui vous prend?*'

I was merely doing what had to be done.

'*Vous êtes complètement piqué!*'

No, not mad, determined. Inspired even. I should have thought of it before. But better late than never. In a quarter of an hour the work was done. Like Pontius Pilate, I washed my hands of the whole business and went back to bed as if nothing had happened. Mum's the word. *Motus et bouche cousue*.

Sunday dawned sunny and fresh. The dappled light from the heart-shaped shutters played on the faded red earthenware tiles. I took a shower, slipped into my elegantly creased off-white linen suit, doffed my dented Panama and went down to the village. The rules clearly stipulate: the jury will examine the garden in the absence of the contestant.

A good kilometre before the village, cars carefully parked on the roadside announced that the fête was already well under way. A distant smell of burning sausages filled the air, mingled with the cabbage-like stink of the beheaded stalks of rape in the nearby fields. The village, normally empty, was full of people and stands, old tables covered in miscellaneous junk – broken Barbie dolls, chipped Kronenbourg beer glasses, gardening magazines from the 1950s, lamps with pink plastic shades.

In the shadow of the church – it was already about twenty-five degrees in the shade – Florence Mabillon and three sharp goats fresh from business school were selling cheese and bonsai vegetables. A fourth goat, ostensibly bored by the whole business, ate *Le Monde* and picked its nose. Florence was reading a book. She was lost in her world, not deigning to look up at the potential customers who passed.

'*Bonjour, Florence.*'

I didn't dare speak in English for fear of unleashing a wave of despair. Her mass of red hair tumbled in cascades on to the delicate pale skin of her shoulders. She stood to serve a tourist in socks and bumbag. I took a peek at the title: *Madame Bovary*. Page 308. Emma has left for an adulterous weekend with the feckless Léon. They go to the Hôtel de Bourgogne and spend three days in a room with doors and shutters closed. In the evenings they take a row boat to dine on an island. Could Florence be trying to tell me something?

A smell of spit-roasted chicken seeped its way between fantasy and reality. The chickeneer, his face red with Rabelaisian bonhomie, was rustling up trade, shouting across the village square for the ladies to come and admire his drumsticks. His wife, pale, fragile, pained and beautiful, stood by him, totally out of place in the chamber of horrors. Our eyes met.

'*Monsieur?*'

Her voice was soft but weary.

'*Vous désirez?*'

It's you I desire, Marie-Laure; I want to snatch you away, to release you from your poultry existence, shackled to the spit. But it was difficult to make such a declaration in the middle of the afternoon when you're supposed to be buying a chicken.

'*Une aile, s'il vous plaît.*'

They don't sell wings.

'*Une cuisse, peut-être.*'

Une cuisse! Une cuisse! My kingdom for a thigh. Our
eyes meet again. There passes between us a fugitive moment
of understanding. I can see Marie-Laure in my white-walled
flat in Donges eating crumpets and reciting irregular verbs.

Bip-bip.

It's Laetitia and her dimples! I long to tell her of my
subscriptions, to thank her for my knowledge of unfranked
penny blacks. But she is with a rather obtuse-looking young
man dressed in garish shoes and baggy trousers. He caresses
the nape of her neck as she talks to me. The gesture is
repugnant; this is no way to treat a replacement postman.
A second car thrusts its way through the crowd. People
peer inside. Ariane Tricot sits in the back reducing Brice,
her cultural attaché of a husband, to the role of chauf-
feur. When she descends from the car in her tight, slit linen
skirt the village holds its breath. Florence, surrounded by
glowering goats, stares intently at Ariane. I introduce
them.

'*Madame . . .*'

'*Madame . . .*'

A moment of cold politeness. They instinctively examine
each other's skin, scouring the surface in search of a
blemish. Their mutual suspicion is most flattering. I explain
that they are both my pupils.

'Anozzer pupil? *Maï-quel.* I did not know!'

I correct the pronunciation. They are still on the blemish
trail.

'Neizzer did I.'

The goat reading *Le Monde* peers over the top of his
paper. Sex is more interesting than politics. I am in an
emotional turmoil. All the women in my life are assembled on the main square of Toison. The excitement is
tinged with a delicious feeling of treachery. Of course, yes,
English girls do have their plus points. My sentimental
card index is full of jodhpurs, of pastor's daughters with

prying tongues behind the oak doors of the presbytery, of ponytails, pigtails, buns and dreadlocks. But I seem to have turned a page. It's not that the English rose has lost her edge. No. It's more a question of vocabulary. I won't be requiring 'darling', 'sweetie pie' or 'honey bunch' any more. I want *'mon chéri'*; I want *'mon amour'*, I would even settle for *'mon cornichon doré'*. The golden gherkin has chosen his camp.

The huge loudspeakers on the wonky stage, planted rather precariously on a series of metal trestles, begin to broadcast stompy folk music. The master of ceremonies – a florid-faced young man with greasy hair and a glittering crimson jacket – announces the arrival of the star entertainers: *Les Berrichons*, a dancing group from the Berry.

The Berry – a *département* south of the Touraine – is famous for witchcraft. Sorcerers lurk in every copse and village, so the legend goes. Unfortunately no one seemed to have bewitched the *Berrichons*, composed of a handful of arthritic grandparents in clogs and a sprinkling of plump Lolitas in headscarves, who started going through the routine of curtseying, bowing and turning, like a bunch of superannuated dervishes. One of Florence's goats, a rather unsophisticated specimen with bulging eyes, is enchanted with the whole thing. *Tant mieux.*

Brice, accompanied by Gossard, is doing a tour of the cattle pens, chatting with the herdsmen and patting rumps. Ariane manages to slip away. She takes me by the arm.

'*Maï-quel.* We shall 'ave a cup of tea togezzer in ze café.'

I hadn't seen Ariane since the firework display. There were a host of questions queuing up in my mind begging for an answer. But the Toison d'Or was too public a place to enquire as to why she had graced me with the wonderful shovel that had lit up my night sky. And I could hardly begin to explain the *merguez* in my pocket under the mocking gaze of the Argonauts.

'*Un thé, s'il vous plaît. Un thé parfumé si possible.*'

Tea? Perfumed tea?

No one had ever asked for tea in the Toison d'Or before. A ripple of excitement runs along the zinc where the assembled piss-artists pause, savouring the very word. Tea. Now what can tea taste like? La Veuve Cognette is delighted. At last someone has asked for a distinguished beverage. She has served eight hundred thousand gallons of Pernod in the last fifty years but now she feels vindicated. It was worth waiting for. She will change the sign outside. *Adieu* café, *bonjour* tea room. She even manages to find a teapot.

The Argonauts are fascinated by the object and make their first hesitant steps in English.

'Tipote.'

'Ze tipote.'

They sniff a teabag and pass it around from bulbous nose to bulbous nose.

'Tibague.'

'Ze tibague.'

Do they come in Chinon?

Ariane finds me tense. With good reason. Fireworks apart, my garden is at this very moment in the process of being inspected by the jury. Ariane is at her most relaxed. She is happy to be a public personage, smiling, gracious, attentive, keen to please all around her. I prefer the private Ariane. I am about to tell her so when there is a noise of distant thunder. The weather hasn't changed. It is simply the arrival of the *Berrichons* in their clogs come to wet their whistle and go to the loo. Brice returns to fetch his wife. His manner is cool – does he suspect me of illicit pyrotechnics?

The electrical system crackles into life again and beckons us to assemble around the flag of Venezuela in front of the Mairie. The jury have returned and have come to their decision. The hour of reckoning is upon us. The suspense is almost unbearable. It takes an inordinate amount of

time to heave Madame Roubaud and her Zimmer frame
up on to the stage. Brice Tricot waits at the microphone.
Gossard passes him the cup: a vast plastic urn in imitation gold and marble, about three feet high. The mayor
has to displace his red, white and blue official scarf in
order to take a neatly folded envelope from his inside
pocket. He hands it to Brice, who opens it.

'The winner of this year's annual garden festival competition is . . .'

I am about to faint, my heart beating fast and loud.
Brice, a master of drama, passes the paper in turn to his
beautiful wife. Ariane takes it, reads, smiles, brushes a
wayward lock of hair from her eyes, and with the sensu-
ality of Marilyn Monroe wishing her President a happy
birthday, takes the microphone.

'The cup this year is awarded to . . .'

My beating heart apart, you could hear a pin drop. The
village, already split by the street-name war, already given
to mutilating benches and pumpkins, prepares itself for
yet another injustice, for yet another reason for strife and
tension. Gossard is white. This is a red Gaviscon alert.

'To . . . Monsieur Sadler! *Maï-quel.*'

To me? I've won. I've done it. My dream has come true.
It is incredible. But curiously the announcement of my
success comes as an anti-climax. I would almost have been
more excited if I had lost.

Polite applause.

I clamber on to the stage. Before me a sea of congrat-
ulatory but rather stunned faces. Ariane hands me the cup,
her fingers under the plastic base licentiously stroking my
own as she hands it to me and kisses me chastely on each
cheek. If only there was darkness so that I could belat-
edly return the firework compliment – but this is no place
for a *patin*. The jury shake me by the hand and pat me
on the back. In turn, I take a scrappy piece of folded paper
out of my *merguez* pocket and, edging my way as close

as possible to Madame Roubaud's right armpit, prepare
to make a public announcement. Silence falls.

'*Monsieur l'attaché culturel; Madame, Monsieur le
Maire; mesdames, mesdemoiselles, messieurs . . .*'

I had written it all down just in case.

'This distinction both honours and delights me. It is of
course the fruit of a certain amount of hard labour . . .
La terre est basse . . .'

And the assembled company repeat after me as in church:
'*La terre est basse.*'

'But I would like to take this public opportunity, at a
moment when the village of Toison, in granting its highest
honour to a *rosbif*, to a representative of its eternal enemy,
shows itself to be truly European, to say that, on behalf
of the nation, we are desperately sorry for having done
what we did to Joan of Arc.'

I thought they might find me witty. Nothing of the kind.
Polite applause greets the end of my speech. The village
seems more interested in how the losers are going to react.
Ariane gives me another chaste public kiss. I would like
to think that she squeezed my hand but I'm not sure that
she did. The official car arrives at the foot of the stage
and Brice and Ariane are whisked off to another function,
waving to the crowd as they leave. I wave in turn, forlornly
watching the car disappear over the brow of the hill
beyond the cemetery. Will I ever see Ariane again? Is this
adieu?

The climax over, the fête starts to pack up. Crying brats
are carted back to the Peugeot, stands are folded, junk
lovingly stored away in wooden crates. Three sardonic
goats wave a hoof from the back of their lorry.

'*Salut, Maï-quel!*'

'*Au revoir, Maï-quel!*'

'*Et encore bravo, Maï-quel!*'

Mr Chicken has for once sold everything. There are no
leftovers. A last-minute rush on his thighs means that

tonight they can eat fish. The relief is palpable on Marie-Laure's once pale cheeks, now flushed pink with pleasure at the thought of salmon. Dirty papers fly over the roof of the church as a wind gets up.

I walk back alone to the Mazda. Difficult to walk casually when you're carrying a bulky trophy. I should brandish it over my head, drink champagne from it, kiss it on my knees. But no one seems to take any notice of me. I slip it under my arm and carefully wedge it like a squid in the boot of the Mazda, making sure it is firmly closed. Any exhibitionism would clearly be frowned upon.

No. I am wrong. Someone is looking at me. Aimé Matou has followed me back to the car. Even at a distance of some twenty yards his mood is palpable. He doesn't understand what has happened. He wants to speak to me. How did I do it? Why did I win? Why wasn't it him? How is it that this upstart *rosbif* can cruise in and win the much-coveted plastic cup? Everyone knows his was the best garden. Everyone knows he is the best gardener. I can see what he's thinking. Was it because I am a friend of the Tricot? Because I plant my leeks with a pneumatic drill? Was I a compromise candidate to stop further divisions in the village?

He gazes at the boot firmly closed on the prize which should rightfully be his. I put my arm around his shoulder. The gesture is risky. *Aimé le paysan* could think me condescending, or gay, or both. But no. He seems to understand my compassion. I invite him back to the house.

'*Aimé. Venez à la maison.*'

I'll explain the secret.

Aimé follows me in his orange Renault 12. We arrive and go down immediately to the bottom of the garden. He's just got to know. I turn, a little shamefaced, and indicate the leek patch, the key to my success. Aimé looks at the leeks in silence. He turns pale. He understands. He has met his match. Not in gardening skill, not in any green-fingered artistry. No. Even he, the ultimate French peasant, has met his match in cunning.

On Sunday morning, just before the fête, I had risen very early. Driven by a desire for victory I had made a daring decision. I had gone down to the bottom of the garden in the warm half-light of dawn, I had dug up my horrified leeks and I had replanted them to read

V–I–V–E L–A F–R–A–N–C–E

Aimé bows his head in wonder.

Ces Angliches. They'll stop at nothing.

We sit on the wall in the evening breeze, a glass of *gnôle* in our hands, the plastic trophy alongside us and we chink glasses.

'*Tchin.*'

'*Tchin, Aimé.*'

And together we get plastered in order to re-cement the *entente cordiale*.

23

One day it is summer; the next, autumn.

With the change in the season comes a change in the light. The deep colours of the sky become less intense, as if a drop of milk had been spilt in a cup of blue tea. Contours are clearer and sharper. Trees and shrubs no longer vibrate in the white-hot afternoon air. The countryside is still, as if frozen in the pure air. Shadows are longer, morning mists slower to dissolve. If you walk barefoot in the grass, the dew is cold enough to give you a headache. The hornbeam hedge swaps its August green for September brown. The sunflowers, long past their prime, are spindly brown stalks with burned-out hats. The soundtrack changes along with the colours. On the distant slope of field, with its neatly etched furrows, a tractor imperceptibly grinds forward. A chainsaw echoes in the forest as if a mad dentist had a surgery up a tree. A trailor clatters on the road carrying cubic metres of winter wood. Chattering birds begin to congregate on the telephone lines. What the hell are the swallows going to do when mobiles rule the world? In the evening I grill a few chestnuts on the open fire in a specially contrived frying pan with holes in it. A chestnut, a glass of *bernache* – the first, half-fermented pressing of the grapes. It slips down like fresh fruit juice. It's only when you've finished the bottle that you realise it wasn't.

From the Atac catalogue, after a careful adding-up of my points, I have at last selected my gift. I decide to forgo the fondue set decorated with a Swiss mountain scene because this would encourage me to eat an inordinate amount of melted cheese, and chose instead a blue metal box containing a repair kit: screwdrivers, adjustable spanners, ring spanners and a socket set. I have never repaired anything in my life. But once back in Abesbury, in a fit of depression born of my desire not to be there, I shall, thanks to my DIY kit, be able to dismantle my rented thatched cottage with some savagery before returning to Dover.

The supermarket shelves are packed with equipment for the new school term: rucksacks, pencil cases, blocks of paper. *La rentrée* – back to school – is a terrible reminder plastered on hoardings everywhere. *Je ne veux pas rentrer.* I don't want to leave. As things stand, my six months are ending untidily. Florence Mabillon, doubtless influenced by her praetorian guard of fawning goats, finds me a disappointment; Ariane has driven off to new adventures and Marie-Laure, at least for the moment, is happy with her salmon steak. I am going to pack everything into the Mazda, slam the fickle boot for the last time and head off down the drive without Aimé Matou's cows even deigning to acknowledge my departure. Is this to be the pattern of my life? Forever forced to go back home?

I sleep badly. Around four in the morning, after an endless search for a cool and restful corner of my pummelled pillow, I get up and open the window. I freeze. A shudder runs down my spine. From the depths of the dark forest behind Aimé's battered farm, a terrifying guttural roar of desire and pain emerges, as if from the beginning of time.

Le brame. The atavistic cry of a stag on heat. Belling or troating, says the dictionary. I know how you feel, old chum. That makes two of us. And from the comfort of my double-glazed *brame*-proof Velux I join in the chorus. If ever Aimé is on rump patrol in the middle of the night he's going to witness a unique sight: a *rosbif* at his attic window, troating to the moon.

Two weeks before my final departure a particular honour comes my way – an invitation to join the Argonauts for the *ouverture de la chasse* – the opening of the hunting season. That the *chasse* was soon to be upon us had been evident for some time from the fact that the village had swapped summer acrylic for Vietnam-style flak jackets smelling of mothballs. At dusk hunting horns rehearse 'O Sole Mio' in the echoing courtyards of distant farmyards. The local dogs sense the growing excitement, practising barking from eleven at night to three o'clock in the morning.

Hunting – or shooting, to be more precise – has become a very sophisticated activity in the canton of Toison, following the virtual annihilation of all living animals by the extremely efficient hunts of previous years. The fact that there is nothing to shoot makes the sport even more exciting. The *tableau de chasse* – traditionally the proud display of numerous dead animals at the end of the hunt – is now distributed as a castlist before the season begins.

If I have understood correctly, for slaughtering this year on the commune of Toison we have some thirty-six pre-selected birds and animals including twelve battery-farm pheasants – who have never flown before and who have been given lessons by Nestor the baker; seven partridges – six cocks and a hen, whom Tubard has met and apparently found charming; a handful of lazy rabbits for the beginners; an extremely fit hare, left over from last season and who wears a medal to commemorate the fact; four guineafowl, who are extremely surprised to be elevated to the status of game but who assume the situation with resignation ever since they escaped from Monsieiur Séguy's coop; and, last but not least, a badger, included on the list as a special guest simply to please Le Père Jules whose vision, hampered by the position of his orange crash helmet, means that he can shoot only large animals at close quarters.

At first I attempt to refuse the honour of joining the Argonauts, pleading the fact that I have really nothing suitable to wear. Unfortunately Madame Coudray, who is a widow, comes up trumps. She has kept her late husband's hunting gear in a plastic bag in the wardrobe. The fact that he was a dwarf does not deter my new friends. The camouflage jacket, army bob cap and cartridge shoulder belt suit me to a T. I look at myself in the mirror. Tight but virile. Wildlife beware.

Rendezvous is given at the Toison d'Or at eight in the morning for the stirrup cup – *le coup de l'étrier*. Softened up by the booze, all seven of us and our gunbelts cram into a battered Renault 4 which immediately sinks, like one of Serge Leroi's excavators, into the soft mud of the track leading into the forest. The idea of spending the whole day extracting the vehicle from the quagmire has the edge over annihilating animals and I leap gamely from the car, quietly tugging as the others push. Sadly, even a full-size *rosbif* can do nothing pitted against six walruses and the Renault is debogged without any fuss.

The hunting lodge is a wooden shack, hand-built and designed by the fraternity. This is clear when Denis, in a passing moment of imbalance, leans on the window sill and the whole caboodle collapses. No one is perturbed, and we all have another slug as we put the puzzle back together again. Things get serious with the arrival of Louis in his green van, its trailer chock-full of slavering hounds. Louis is a refuse collector. His pack eat what he finds in the local dustbins. The dogs are extremely well fed but all suffer from appalling halitosis.

Itchy trigger fingers are soothed thanks to a few cool bottles of young Chinon, which we drink as Tubard prepares a *coq au vin*. I follow the chef to the kitchen – an old, rickety table leaning against the back wall of the shack – on to which three bottles of oil, vinegar and mustard are stuck by a glue made of the remains of a three-year-old *boeuf bourguignon*. Tubard opens four huge preserve jars, pours the contents into a rusty saucepan and lights the Butagaz. The flame leaps into the air, splutters and fades, so we prepare to eat our *coq* cold. I offer to nip to Super U to replace the gas bottle. In vain. Chinon and camaraderie provide the warmth the gas refused us.

After an extremely runny Camembert, which Nestor threatens to riddle with bullets if it won't keep still, we get our eye in by shooting at a makeshift target nailed to a tree – a dangerous sport as Penthouse was relieving himself in the vicinity. He could have ended up on the wall in the place of the antlers. There followed a series of risqué jokes about his *zizi* being stuffed by a taxidermist and displayed for all to see on the walnut sideboard.

Folded neatly in each pocket, the list of this year's permitted game. Nestor, who knows the pheasant intimately having provided the take-off instructions, describes him. He has a slight limp and a light blue feather in his bum. We take note. It is essential not to kill the wrong birds. This is all part of the sport. You nobble the wrong one and you're out. In the course of his explanation Roger fires off in the direction of Denis and misses him with real skill.

The *sous-bois* – the undergrowth – crackles beneath the inexorable advance of the camouflaged game brigade. Shots ring out left, right and centre. After the lull of lunch we are keyed up, ready for blood. It is, however, difficult to focus. A gnat close-up could be a distant partridge. The woods resound to the death rattle of flies and mosquitoes. The other test is not to kill each other. This is not as simple as it might at first seem. Wearing flecked green and brown combat gear we look very much like the scavengers we are trying to eliminate. In this respect the

Argonauts are masterful. Tubard misses Jules, Denis misses Roger, Pois-Chiche misses Denis by inches – a very impressive shot.

An exciting moment – a distant sound of wings beating the air. There, above us, a flight of wild ducks. The dogs look up, their eyes full of savage dreams. Instinctively we raise our barrels and fire *boom boom* into the air – at three French airforce fighter planes also travelling over our heads but at some 800 kilometres an hour. Fortunately no direct hit is recorded. Military aircraft are not on the list for this year.

Towards the end of the afternoon a laconic boar makes a visit. You can't fool him. He knows only too well that he's on next year's list. What a tease! We level our guns at him and go *pan pan*, which is the noise French guns make. The boar farts and lumbers off to take the piss out of another bunch of *chasseurs*.

At dusk Louis sounds the end of the hunt. We all meet up in a clearing in the middle of the forest, in which there is a circle of seven flamboyantly tumescent red and white spotted poisonous mushrooms. With no stag to dismantle, deprived of innards, we fire at the mushrooms, ripping them to shreds. *Ah, les salauds!* We all feel much better. This is what Aristotle refers to as catharsis.

The Englishman has passed the test with flying colours. My friends gather in a circle around me, pour seven fat glasses of an extremely pungent *gnôle*, pass me the largest glass and sing the ritual song:

> *Ami Michael, Ami Michael*
> *Lève ton verre*
> *Et surtout ne le renverse pas.*

I have to lift the glass to the forehead – *le frontibus*; the chin – *le mentibus*, and then down to the *zigounette*:

Et porte le
Au frontibus
Au mentibus
Au sexibus

And the song ends with the chorus singing in rhythm for as long as it takes me to down the *gnôle* in one draught – '*Et glou et glou et glou et glou . . .*' – saluting me when the glass is finally empty:

> *Il est des nôtres*
> *Il a bu son verre comme les autres!*

My guts feel as if they have been ripped open. Now I know how the stag feels. It's a fitting end to a wonderful day.

So as not to lose face, we drop into Pois-Chiche's house on the way back to the Toison d'Or. He has a wild rabbit – *un lapin de garenne* – in his freezer. We unfreeze it using a hair-drier, stuff it in the trophy bag and look a bit less gormless when we troop into the bar.

Late in the evening, staggering home, I can just make out from the depths of the forest, a chorale composed of twelve pheasants, a hare, several rabbits, Le Père Jules' badger and the inimitable high-pitched tones of the guineafowl thumbing their noses and singing the song that French kids sing to crow over an easy victory:

> *On a gagné! Les doigts dans le nez.*
> *Ils ont perdus! Les doigts dans le cul.*

24

Quite out of the blue, Brice Tricot rings me up. He is most affable.

'Michael?'

I am surprised both by the call and by the tone. After the fireworks I would have suspected more suspicion. I, in turn, am most affable, using exclamation marks normally reserved for Laetitia.

'Brice!'

'Michael. If by any remote chance you happen to be free on Saturday evening, we would like to invite you to a party.'

They know that I am soon heading back to England. They would like to extend an invitation to a fancy-dress ball and concert given by a friend who makes false teeth in his big house in a village not far from Tours.

This is really most charming of them. I am thrilled at the thought of being able to see Ariane one last time. And I am tickled by the irony. My first departure for France was celebrated by a fancy-dress party in Abesbury. My present departure from France is to be fêted in the same fashion. *Ironie du sort*. A quirk of fate.

I am fulsome in thanking Brice for not having forgotten me. A problem now presents itself, however. What am I going to wear?

In reading the press, an illumination. I opened Sophie Hodge's wardrobe with trepidation. A wardrobe is a hive of eroticism. Saint Preux in Rousseau's *La Nouvelle Héloïse* spends a most agreeable afternoon locked up in his girl-friend's closet. I have no intention of climbing into the sweet-smelling sarcophagus, I simply want to borrow a dress, a handbag and, if possible, a pair of gloves.

Sophie Hodge and I are more or less the same size, although her feet are bigger than mine. The flowery dress was perfect, *idem* the crocodile handbag, but the shoes were hopeless. At Emmaus, a French Oxfam depot in a Nissen hut off the Tours–Loches main road, a pair of pink satin high-heeled pumps caught my eye. It was difficult trying them on. I was surrounded by sharp dealers who would be only too quick to suss out the plump Englishman trying on a pair of ladies' shoes. I had to hide them under an enamel bath and hang about waiting for the coast to clear. Final ingredient. In a joke shop – the wonderfully named *magasin de farces et attrapes* – I found a blue rinse wig. We were in business.

On Saturday morning I tried my make-up.

Bip bip!

Bernard looked at me in horror. I was wearing ruby lipstick and a light foundation. His prejudices were confirmed. The English were at it again. In order to provide further satisfaction I puckered my lips in his driving mirror.

'*Je n'ai pas un peu débordé avec le rouge, Bernard?*'

Have I smudged my lipstick? Bernard reversed down the drive at 100 kilometres an hour. Blood pressure 180/250. Revenge is sweet.

Brice Tricot suggested that we take our own cars, but that we meet up at the Reignac crossroads – did I know the labyrinth, he asked, without innuendo. I could then follow them to the party – the house was not easy to find. Once again, with great consideration, they were waiting for me. I began to have a feeling that they were sorry to see me go. Their car had tinted windows. Impossible to see what their fancy dress was.

Driving in high heels was tricky but I did still have time

to admire the beauties of the Touraine countryside. You cross a rather nondescript plain bathed in the delicate pastel light of a huge evening sky and suddenly you wind down into a secret valley full of rivers, hidden castles and troglodyte cottages emerging from the chalk cliffs as if a sculptor had left his work unfinished. As I followed the large Mercedes of Ariane and Brice I began to have a feeling of *déjà vu*. Odd. Had I been here before? That post office, that *auberge*, that bend, they all seemed to recall memories I couldn't place.

Just a minute.

There's a crossroads after that lake. You turn right, left. And then there's a mill. The premonition became almost oppressive. A sign at the entrance to the village should confirm my suspicions. There's a young man leaning against it, flirting with a girl on a solex. At the last minute he moves to the right.

Pont de Ruan.

Ce n'est pas possible!

It was here, in Pont de Ruan, that I had spent a New Year *réveillon* chez Edith and Roland Delluc.* It was here that I had begun to seduce the exquisite, the exotic, the treacherous Madame Delluc by playing the truth game and making chips. Nostalgia lassoes me behind the knees. Nostalgia tinged with a *soupçon* of suffering. I'd like to relive those moments. Go through them all again, pain included.

Brice was waiting for me round the next bend and I nearly drove into them. They made signs. Everything OK? Now is hardly the time to explain. I tried to delete memories from the hard disk, concentrating on following Brice around the village from my past. Right, right, right again, then left into an imposing car park full of expensive dentists' cars drawn up in front of a beautiful house.

* See *An Englishman in Paris* (Pocket Books, 2003).

Le Moulin Delluc.

The coincidence is extraordinary. I have twice been invited to the self-same house tucked away in a secret corner of the Touraine countryside. Did Edith and Brice know each other? Was I going to see Edith again? Hadn't they said a party given by a friend who makes dentures? Roland Delluc was in sugar, not teeth. I am confused.

My heart is beating fast. The door of the mill opens. Edith comes out to greet us. She is wearing her tight waisted jacket and her exotic satin harem trousers. I open my eyes. This woman is not Edith. She is wearing a heavy dress in what looks like velvet furnishing fabric. Brice introduces me. Ariane must have gone on ahead. My legs are shaky. The emotion is too much. The mistress of the house, doubtless the wife of the denture magnate, looks at me oddly, sensing that something is amiss. My face must betray my feelings. I pull myself together and thank her graciously for the invitation. My courtesy does not appear to dissipate the anxious look in her eyes. She asks me to follow her. The concert is being given in a garden at the back of the house.

I don't need instructions. I know the way. I know the garden only too well. There's a path at the bottom. A path I took to buy the eggs at Saturnin's farm. The garden gives on to the millstream. On to le *bief*. I'd learned the word, and had never been able to use it since.

'Le *bief*.'

'*Oui, le bief*.'

The velvet armchair looks at me, her worst suspicions confirmed. Why does he keep repeating 'millstream'?

We enter the house. The smell of the place is overwhelming. It hasn't changed at all. I have to sit down for a moment. Surely this is the same sofa? I put my handbag on a mahogany table. And this the same table? The pouffes and the lampshades are identical. I feel like a stranger at home. Behind that oak door, the kitchen with the huge

American fridge where I had hidden my *tripes à la mode de Caen*. Through the window a glimpse of the distant lake where we'd been duck shooting. And everywhere that smell, the perfume of wood smoke and furniture polish which conjured up the presence of Edith. She is here. In front of me. I am so pleased to see her again. She speaks gently to me.

'*Ça ne va pas?*'

'*Ça va, Edith, merci.*'

The mistress of the house clearly thinks I'm a nutter.

'My name is Sylvie. If you don't feel well perhaps . . .'

She speaks to me in English, in an attempt to humour me. Brice and Ariane have disappeared. In order to set Sylvie's mind at rest, I explain the situation. I have been here before. I had been a friend, indeed a close friend, of the owners. Sylvie explains that she and her husband had never met the previous proprietors. All had been arranged by the estate agents. It was all much more efficient and in the end cost-effective because . . .

I couldn't give a fart. Where are they?

Sylvie has no idea. In Paris? In Switzerland perhaps? She believes they had a house in Switzerland. I put her right. No. They had a beautiful house on the Ile de Ré. Clearly Sylvie, in turn, couldn't give a tinker's about the real-estate assets of the past owners. She's got a party on her hands. With a slight hesitation she gestures in the direction of the loo. Would I like to refresh myself?

Why did she hesitate? I stand and catch my reflection in the mirror. *Nom d'un chien!* In the emotional turmoil I'd quite forgotten. I'd come to the party disguised as Margaret Thatcher, *la dame de fer en personne*.

A guest in a dinner jacket, purporting to fetch a travelling rug from the car, crosses the large drawing room in which the former Prime Minister is regaining her spirits.

'*Bonsoir, madame.*'

He is followed by his wife, who has clearly come for a

peek herself. An appalling thought hits me. Brice, just like
the travelling rug, was wearing a DJ. Sylvie is wearing her
armchair dress. The gawping Bimbo is in a party frock.
This is not a fancy-dress party. I've been fooled, hood-
winked, duped, kippered, taken for a ride. This a party.
A straightforward dentists' binge. Only, as a special attrac-
tion, in the middle of it all, we have the extraordinary one
and only transvestite *rosbif*, the man who thought he was
Margaret Thatcher.

Merci Brice. Merci beaucoup. So that's why you were
so smarmy.

Nothing for it. I'll have to face the crowd. I can't spend
the whole evening cowering on the canapé. It would hardly
be in character. As I appear at the top of the flight of steps
leading down into the garden, the evening air is full of
the sound of gallic nudging. *Ah! Ces Anglais.* What a
nation. What a nerve. They really take the biscuit. *Ils sont
impayables!* Of course, that's what happens if you send
your son to a public school. *Quelle éducation.* But can
you blame them. I mean. The libido will out. Nudge nudge.

I make a decision. If they want Margaret, then they
shall have her. With grace and aplomb, taking care not to
catch my hem in my high heels, I trip down the steps and
make my way towards the stage which has been erected
at the bottom of the garden – away from the roar of the
bief – taking care to do as much damage to the lawn as
I can with my Emmaus pumps. A Yorkshire terrier has a
go at my ankles, the little sod, and I kick him in the balls.
Wonderful what you can do unseen under a skirt.

'*Bonsoir, madame.*'

It's the smug specialist with the *danseuse*. I give him a
smacker under the side whiskers. That'll teach him for
flirting with power.

We all make ourselves ready for the concert. Neat little
progammes are folded on each chair. I am sitting next to
a platinum blonde who has to keep crossing her legs she

is laughing so much. The menu is hardly mouthwatering. Baroque from the twee period. Telemann and other minor composers of the same water with names like Glockenstop. Jolly rhythms for fat Schloss owners. Music for dentists' waiting rooms. Nothing to get your teeth into. Amorosa should try her hand at composing.

A man in a dinner jacket next to me oozes charm.

'I just love *Tafelmusik*. And you, madame?'

'Bores the knickers off me, darling.'

Margaret is on form tonight.

Five retired musicians from the symphony orchestra of Loches have formed a baroque ensemble. They balance their scores on the spindly stands, secure their violins under their triple chins, shake the spit from the flutes and we're off. After four bars you need a drink. It's jolly, polite, pert – and a pain in the arse. The insipid brew is poured into the assembled ears like lukewarm tea. They close their eyes to simulate ecstasy but they are either going off to sleep or eyeing the miniskirt of the waitress. Every four minutes or so they turn round and nod as if to say – did you catch that modulation? How about that for a reprise? But no one is taken in. They are bored out of their minds. Occasionally, in between movements, I squeeze the knee of the Dinner Jacket and give a wink. *Tafelmusik* must turn me on. He begins to look nervous.

The best part is the bat. Everyone loves the bat, a brother or sister of the piss-artist from my cellar who flies in low, eliciting cries of horror from the ladies who throw their hands above their head to protect their hair. This results in acriminious '*chut*' – shush – from the baroque aficionados whose concentration is impaired. I make matters worse by rustling my skirt. *Chut!* So I lift them even higher and give a *fortissimo* rustle. *CHUT!* We all love '*chut*-ing'. Far better than listening to the baroque treacle ensemble.

The guests are keen to know my reaction at the end of the concert.

'And how did you find the music, madame?'

'*Chiante.*'

Ha ha. She really is a card. But they are a little on edge.

'You would have preferred . . . ?'

'Give me the Stones any day.'

They are taken aback but, at the same time, enchanted. They really go for Margaret. What a pity France has never had *une dame de fer*. She'd have put the shop in order.

'A little sangria?'

'I'll have some Bolly, *mon chou*, if you don't mind.'

Ariane slips away from a group engrossed in a riveting conversation about fillings. Until now she has been keeping her distance. Was she party to all this? Did Brice take her into his confidence?

'*Maï-quel . . .*'

I must resist.

'Yes, Ariane?'

'*Ça vous va très bien, vous savez . . .*'

Does she fancy me in drag? Ariane's eyes are burning coals. I am transported back to the labyrinth. Imaginary fireworks explode in my buccal cavity.

'*Et moi?*'

She looks immensely desirable.

'*Aussi belle que traîtresse, Ariane.*' As beautiful as you are treacherous.

'*Maï-quel!*'

She is astounded. Bowled over. *Sur le cul.*

'*Vous êtes gonflé, Maï-quel.*'

No. It's not me who is daring, darling. It's Margaret. Remember the Falklands.

Ariane seems to have stumbled upon a new *Maï-quel*. She is flirtatious and peckish, and suggests that we have a little intimate nibble together. *Une collation à deux.* I send her off to the fridge to look for some caviar, arrange to meet her behind the stage at the bottom of the garden and shut myself away in the bathroom.

And what was written came to pass.

My desire was to get away from it all. But the gods, reclining on their bed of clouds with ambrosial indigestion, had obviously decided otherwise. They wanted to have some fun. Or, uncharacteristically, they wanted to reward perseverance.

Int. Night. Bathroom.

Toc toc

Ariane and the sturgeon roe? I hesitate. Then, with little enthusiasm: '*Oui.*'

'*Ouvrez, s'il vous plaît.*'

The voice is soft, attractively contralto. It is certainly not Ariane. I open the door.

'I've brought you this.'

She has dark eyes and dark hair, a mass of curls tumbling on to her lean bronzed shoulders. She is wearing a white silk T-shirt. On a tray she is carrying Kleenex, make-up remover, a pullover and a bottle of Chinon.

'*Je vous démaquille.*'

I would be only too delighted to have my make-up removed. But why does she want to?

'I've just had a row. My ex won't dream of looking for me here. I deflated the tyres of his car.'

Perhaps, once we've finished with the cold cream, we can do Brice's. With immense care and attention, she sets about returning me to my original state. My eyes are closed. From time to time I take a swig of Chinon. I can sense her close to me. She asks what I thought of the concert. I start to knock the baroque and to lay into Telemann but she suggests that I shouldn't get het up over trifles. She caresses my eyelids with a moist pad.

'*Un moment.*'

And she is gone. I look at myself in the mirror. Happily, the work is only half done. She returns with a *saucisson*, a baguette and a lamp. Without the neon over the wash-basin, the bathroom is bathed in a softer light.

'*C'est mieux ainsi.*'

She cuts the sausage with a Swiss Army knife from her handbag. I close my eyes again and let her take over. Once again I can feel her very close to me, her hair brushing against my cheek. What do I think of the *saucisson*? Delicious. She tells me she brought it back from the Auvergne, where she'd been karting with her ex. I tell her I prefer *saucisson* to karting. Her long delicate fingers move from my eyes to my chin, cheeks, ears and round to the back of my neck. Did I put make-up on the back of my neck?

'*Attendez.*'

And she's gone again. There's some cold cream in the corner of my left eye and I give it a quick rub which immediately makes it smart. My eyes are closed when she returns.

'*Ouvrez les yeux.*'

She is holding a dusty old bottle. A Vouvray *moelleux* 1947. 1947! The year of the century. The best sweet wine the Loire has ever made. The kind of booze you have to drink on your knees – and it turns up in a bathroom!

'My ex brought it. But he's mean. He hid it in the boot. *On va la boire!*'

She takes a corkscrew out of her bag – clearly a Hermès version of my Super U tool kit – and opens it. I watch her lithe arms as she slowly pulls the cork. She smiles as it pops, a smile to melt the knees of a concrete garden gnome.

'*Goûtez.*'

I close my eyes. The wine is light and dense, fresh and deliquescent, green and autumnal. I have never tasted anything so delicious. This is the best moment I have ever spent in a bathroom. I open my eyes, look at her and there you are, no questions asked, it happened. Just like that. As simple as falling off a log.

I am in love. *Je suis amoureux.*

Ouf. At last. *Enfin.* I've been waiting for this moment for a long time. I must say I feel a good deal better.

Love at first sight? *Le coup de foudre?* Nothing to it. The following recipe should do the trick: a coincidence, some boring baroque, a *saucisson*, a sentimental bathroom, a jar of cold cream, a bottle of Vouvray '47, *elle et moi.* Infallible.

I lean towards her, slowly, very slowly. Our eyes meet, smile, my lips graze hers, tasting the sugar of the wine and the softness of her kiss. I'm still a bit sticky so she takes a Kleenex to the few remaining nooks and crannies, finishing the job with the tip of her tongue.

Toc toc

There goes the bloody door again. A man's voice. 'Loulou?'

'Are you Loulou?' I whisper.

She nods. And replies.

'*Je ne suis pas là.*'

Was that Monsieur Karting?

'*C'est lui?*'

'*C'était lui.*'

My turn next. Tentative steps arrive at the door.

'*Maï-quel?*'

My knees are made of ice.

'I 'ave found ze caviar.'

'And I, Ariane, love.'

Silence. Understandably so. This is not the kind of sentence you expect to be thrown at you from behind the locked door of a dentist's bathroom. Ariane, I sense, is moved. Her steps fade slowly back down the corridor. I am sad but delighted. The Vouvray has given me a passion for oxymorons.

Using a make-up pencil we each write our addresses on a tissue. I tell her what I've been wanting to say for so long.

'Je vous aime.'

I had to say *vous* becuse I didn't know who she was. I was thrilled to be passionate and correct at the same time.

She gives me a last kiss, expresses very positive surprise at the unexpected excitability of the British, and leaves. On the lawn the baroque ensemble throws caution to the winds and begins to play *Carmen*. Real music at last! Lady Thatcher, at the very peak of her form, sings 'L'amour est enfant de bohème' and dances a flamenco.

I love this country. I love its dentists. I love its dark-haired, sensual, tyre-deflating, Vouvray-swigging make-up removers.

Vive l'amour.
Merci Edith.

25

The beginning of a new term is a difficult moment in the life of a teacher. Facing your colleagues once again after a long break, in the same lecture halls, in the same atmosphere of felt pens, books and polish, is never easy. You park the car in the faculty car park and walk across the tarmac to the acrid-smelling privet-lined walk leading to the library steps. It's the same, but not quite the same. Last year's anoraks and T-shirts are filled with different bodies, different faces, different names. But each autumn the novelty diminishes, the differences become ever more slight, the repetition ever greater.

Not so this year.

It is seven o'clock in the morning on the first day of term. The dawn air is sharp and clear. Carefully tended vines stretch out to the horizon where the vineyard disappears down a far slope leading to the village. Sun-gorged grapes – September was exceptionally hot – glisten in the dew. A bell in the steeple of the church in Vouvray rings the hour. An old man in a *bleu de travail* is walking through the vines carrying *pâté de campagne*, bread and, on a little trolley behind him, a small cask of white. My hands are already stiff from working the secateurs. The grapes have to be harvested bunch by bunch. A sandwich, the bread folded back over a thick slice of pâté, a slug of morning Vouvray: the greatest breakfast since Weetabix.

I have composed a letter to Richard Badger, the unctuous Head of Department, to explain my priorities and my decision. I won't be going back, because I can't. It's as simple as that. *Adieu Swindon*. For reasons upon which, in the course of the present, I would prefer not to expand, I am obliged to remain in France. Yours sincerely.

I had received a brief note from my own private make-up artist. She would, she says, quite simply, be pleased to see me again. *Et moi de même*. If you listen to your heart, life is straightforward. I unbend, squint in the direction of the rising sun, remember Racine and the heartbreaking separation at the end of *Bérénice*:

Dans un mois, dans un an, comment souffrirons-nous,
Seigneur, que tant de mers me séparent de vous?
Que le jour recommence et que le jour finisse
Sans que jamais Titus puisse voir Bérénice,
Sans que de tout le jour je puisse voir Titus[*]

The Queen of Palestine was right. It's not on. Being less under pressure, I have decided not to pack my bags. Exile is not for me. I shall not be kicking at weeds down the waterlogged bottom of my garden in Abesbury, consumed with regret. No sir. Remorse is rust. I shall remain rust-less and not restless.

It's my turn to carry the *hotte*, and I slip the leather straps over my shoulders to collect the grapes from the pickers' baskets. I have to kneel down so that the old ladies in black can reach to pour in their harvest. At the end of the row of vines, the tractor and trailer. I climb the four steps of the ladder and, with a nudge of my shoulder,

---

[*] 'In a month, in a year, how shall we suffer / My lord, when so many seas come between us / To think that a day should begin and that a day should end / Without Titus ever seeing Bérénice / Without Bérénice ever setting eyes on Titus.' *Bérénice*, Act 5: in *Racine for Leeks*.

toss the lot down into the crimson and violet sea of grapes. An incredible smell of heady juice rises from the lake of bunches already half-crushed by their own weight. For a second I look down on to the village wreathed in the morning mist. This is where I want to be. My bottle was half empty. France has topped me up. *Je suis ouillé.* Ullage at last.

I take my resignation letter down to Toison late that evening. The village has settled its squabbles. Brand-new bright blue metal plates proclaim to the world the names of the streets. I walk up la Rue des Roses, turn into the Allée des Primevères, and slip the missive in the postbox Place de France.

Toison is at peace.

Or is it?

Oddly, there are figures lurking in doorways. Pois-Chiche is waiting at the entrance to the café, Henri is sitting on his bench, Gossard I can see in the school play-ground, Penthouse is sitting on the church steps, Tubard is at home with the window open, Jules in his transistor orchard.

What's going on?

What are they waiting for?

I approach Henri to shake his hand.

Dddrrriiinnnggg

What the?!

Dddrrriiinnnggg

Everyone stands. The atmosphere is electric.

Dddrrriiinnnggg

Dddrrriiinnnggg

In the orchard, *Dddrrriiinnnggg. Dddrrriiinnnggg* at the school, *Dddrrriiinnnggg* at the Toison d'Or. *Dddrrriiinnnggg* at the bakers. And then, as if the village were a set of sonorous dominoes, *Dddrrriiinnnggg* in every house.

Cries of joy ring out left, right and centre.

'*Ça y est!*'
'*Enfin!*'
Henri majestically rises on his tightrope.
'*Le réseau, on l'a.*'
Coverage at last! Mobile phones work in the village!
Enfin!
I did well to stay.
Toison is once again the centre of the universe.

POCKET
BOOKS

AN ENGLISHMAN IN PARIS

L'éducation continentale

Michael Sadler
Preface by Peter Mayle

'Wonderfully amusing'
HRH Prince Charles

'A triumph: warmly and insightfully observed;
brilliantly funny' **John Birt**

South coast-born, Parisian *manqué*, Michael
Sadler set out to spend a year in the city of light
to educate himself in the mysterious ways of the
continent. Triple-parking, tasting wine at the
Bon Marché, keeping one's end up at a *dîner
bourgeois*, keeping one's wicket in a *liaison
dangereuse* afterwards – each challenge is
broached with a mixture of distance (British) and
relish (Gallic). Abrasive and tender, naïve and in
the know, *An Englishman in Paris* is a sharp,
hilarious and affectionate look at our nearest
neighbours and the nature of foreignness.

PRICE £6.99
ISBN 0-7434-4046-3